Pictorial Bible Atlas

J Catling Allen

with maps drawn by Malcolm Porter

Hulton

The Bible is the world's most treasured religious book. It is read by millions of people all over the world – particularly by Jews and Christians, but also by people of other religions. For, although the Bible was written so long ago, its message is timeless. Christians believe that God continues to speak to us today through the Bible revealing the truth about himself, and the way we should live. This is why Christians often call the Bible the written Word of God, and believe that God guided and helped the writers to record his message to mankind. Christians therefore call the Bible an 'inspired' book, and claim that it has divine authority.

But the religious message of the Bible cannot be truly understood without some knowledge of its geographical and historical background. The purpose of this Bible atlas, therefore, is to help students understand the Bible better by providing a series of simple maps, accompany-ing texts, and recent photographs to illustrate the geographical and historical setting of the Bible story.

The text relates the maps to the relevant events recorded in the Bible, and places them in their geographical and historical setting. Recent archaeological discoveries are also mentioned in view of their importance to Biblical studies, and Bible references are given where appropriate.

The atlas begins with an introductory section on the Bible and Bible Lands. This is followed by two main sections covering the Old and New Testament periods – summarised by Time Charts – and a short section of two maps showing the spread of Christianity. Finally, there is a section on Archaeology and the Bible concluding with two maps showing important archaeological sites in Bible Lands.

The Middle East from space

Acknowledgements

The author is grateful for the helpful advice and comments on this book received from Miss Elizabeth Moore and Mr Stephen Thompson.
Photographs are reproduced by kind permission of the following: The Israel Museum (p.4 bottom left); BBC Hulton Picture Library (p. 5 top right); British Library (p. 5 bottom left); Paul Jordan (p. 15 top).
NASA (p. 2)
Cover: J. Allan Cash
All the other photographs were taken by the author.

First published 1980 by Hulton Educational Publications Ltd., Raans Road, Amersham, Bucks. HP6 6JJ.

ISBN 0 7175 0857 9

© 1980 John Catling Allen
Maps © 1980 Hulton Educational Publications Ltd
Reprinted 1982

The Bible is a collection of Jewish and Christian sacred writings, or holy scriptures. So, strictly speaking, the Bible is not one book but a collection of books in one volume. In fact, the word 'Bible' comes from the Greek word 'Biblia' which means 'Books'.

These books were written by many different authors in three different languages – Hebrew, Aramaic and Greek – at widely different times between c. 950 B.C. and A.D. 100. Their books are also very different, and contain a wide variety of literature – history and folklore, laws and legends, poems and prayers, proverbs and prophecy, letters and sermons. But, in spite of their diversity, there is an underlying unity running through them. For they all reveal – directly or indirectly – the truth about God and his will for mankind. This is why they were collected and bound together under one cover to form the book we now know as the Bible.

The complete Bible has eighty books which are divided into three sections – the Old Testament, the Apocrypha, and the New Testament. The Old Testament has thirty-nine books. They are the sacred writings of the Jewish people, but Christians also accept them as holy scripture. They were originally written on scrolls either in Hebrew or Aramaic between the 10th and 2nd centuries B.C. Later, they were arranged in three groups – The Law, The Prophets and The Writings.

None of the original Old Testament manuscripts has survived and, until recently, the oldest manuscripts dated from the 10th century A.D. But in 1947 the first Dead Sea Scrolls were discovered at Qumran. Among them were manuscripts of all the Old Testament books

– except Esther – dating from not later than the 1st century A.D. Although they are some thousand years earlier than the 10th century manuscripts, their texts are very similar.

Ancient Scroll of the Pentateuch

Dead Sea Scroll (Old Testament)

The Apocrypha – from a Greek word meaning 'secret' or 'hidden' – forms the second section of the complete Bible, and has fourteen books. They are also Jewish writings. They were originally written either in Hebrew or Greek between the 4th century B.C. and the 1st century A.D. Many of them were added to the Hebrew Old Testament when it was translated into Greek between the 3rd and 2nd centuries B.C. This Greek version of the Old Testament – known as the Septuagint – was used by many Christians in the early days of the Church. But there has always been a difference of opinion amongst Christians as to whether they should be accepted as holy scripture. This is why they are included in some versions of the Bible, but not in others.

The New Testament has twenty-seven books. They were written in Greek by Christians during the 1st and 2nd centuries A.D.

Like the books in the Old Testament, the New Testament books were only gradually collected together to form one volume. In fact, it was not until the 4th century A.D. that the list, or canon, of books to be included in the New Testament was finally decided by the Church. The four Gospels telling the story of Jesus come first. They are followed by the Acts of the Apostles telling the story of the early Church up to about A.D. 62. Then there are twenty-one Letters written by St. Paul and other leading 1st-century Christians. Last of all is The Revelation, a book of visions about God's final victory over evil.

Mediaeval scribe copying the Bible

The exact dating of the New Testament books is uncertain. But Biblical scholars think that St. Paul's early letters were the first to be written. They are dated between A.D. 48 and A.D. 60, that is, before the four Gospels and most of the other books, which are thought to have been written between A.D. 65 and A.D. 100.

Although none of the original New Testament manuscripts has survived, there are many ancient Greek texts in existence. The earliest is a papyrus fragment of St. John's Gospel dating from c. A.D. 125. Among the others is a 4th-century manuscript called the Codex Sinaiticus which contains the complete New Testament. This ancient Codex, or manuscript, was discovered by chance in St. Catherine's Monastery on Mount Sinai in 1844, and is now in the British Museum.

By the middle of the 3rd-century, the New Testament was being translated from early Greek manuscripts into other languages such as Syriac, Coptic and Latin. The first English translation was made in the 14th century when the complete Bible was translated into English for the first time. Known as 'Wycliffe's Bible', it was translated from a 4th-century Latin version called the Vulgate.

After the invention of printing in the 15th century, further English translations were made including the famous King James's or Authorised Version of 1611, which has remained in use up to the present time. Since the last century, however, many new English translations have been made. Among recent ones are the Revised Standard Version, the Jerusalem Bible, and the New English Bible. These, and other modern English versions, are based on the most accurate ancient texts, and take into account the results of modern Biblical scholarship.

Codex Sinaiticus — a 4th century Greek New Testament

Although the story of the Bible is centred on the small land of Palestine, it cannot be understood without reference to the surrounding lands. For, owing to its geographical position, Palestine was greatly influenced in ancient times by the history and culture of the nations surrounding it. The Biblical record of God's revelation, therefore, must be placed in the geographical, historical and cultural context in which it was written.

The importance of Palestine in the history of the ancient world lies in the fact that it is situated in the 'Fertile Crescent' (See map page 8–9). This is the name given to the fertile area around the Arabian desert. It forms a semi-circle from Egypt up through Palestine and Syria, and then follows the Tigris and Euphrates down through Mesopotamia (the 'land between the rivers') to the Persian Gulf.

The Fertile Crescent was an early centre of civilisation because the waters of the rivers Tigris and Euphrates, the Jordan and the Nile made the land fertile. People naturally settled in these regions where there was plenty of water, rich soil, and a hot climate, which enabled them to grow crops and keep animals.

The eastern end of the Fertile Crescent is generally thought to have been one of the earliest centres of civilisation. The Sumerians – a non-Semitic race, who may have come from the east (Gen. 11.2.) – were the first known people to settle here c. 3500 B.C. They founded a kingdom known as Sumer (Biblical Shinar), which consisted of a number of city-states such as Uruk (Biblical Erech), Ur and Eridu. The development of their civilisation and culture has been revealed by excavations on the sites of Sumerian cities in present-day Iraq. At Uruk, for example, archaeologists found hundreds of small clay tablets with a primitive form of picture writing dating from around 3100 B.C., which later developed into wedge-shaped writing known as 'cuneiform'.

The Sumerians continued their settled life until Semitic tribes from the desert invaded the fertile lands north of Sumer and began to attack their cities. By about 2350 B.C., Sargon 1, one of their chieftains, had founded the small kingdom of Akkad and conquered Sumer. He was the first great leader of the Semitic race, and the founder of an empire which stretched from Mesopotamia to the Mediterranean.

Meanwhile, another Semitic empire had been established c. 2400 B.C., in the Fertile Crescent covering the whole of Syria and Palestine. It was a powerful Canaanite empire, and its existence has only recently been discovered as a result of recent excavations at Ebla in northern Syria. (See p. 60). These excavations have also revealed that Sargon's grandson, Narum-Sin of Akkad, conquered Ebla and burnt the city, including the royal palace, c. 2250 B.C. But the Akkadian empire founded by Sargon 1 was brought to an end when people called Gutians descended on the Fertile Crescent from the Zagros mountains c. 2200 B.C.

Junction of Rivers Tigris and Euphrates at Al Qurna, Iraq

The River Nile at Aswan in Egypt

The Fertile Crescent was again invaded by Semitic tribes around 2000 B.C. They were the Amorites of the Old Testament, who came from the Arabian desert and established kingdoms throughout Syria and Mesopotamia. One of them was the kingdom of Babylon whose most famous king was Hammurabi (18th century B.C.). He is noted for his code of laws resembling the later laws of Moses, and was the builder of Babylon's first Ziggurat. This was almost certainly the background for the Tower of Babel story in Genesis 11.1-9. (Babel is the Hebrew for Babylon). Hammurabi also brought the whole of Mesopotamia under his rule, and founded the Old Babylonian Empire. Among the cities he conquered was Mari, the magnificent capital of another Amorite kingdom on the Euphrates. Excavations here have provided Biblical scholars with valuable new information about the possible historical background of the Hebrew Patriarchs.

During the period of the Patriarchs, Syria and Palestine are thought to have been controlled by Egypt, which had been a powerful kingdom for centuries. For the Nile Valley is very fertile, and people settled here in the earliest times. Then, around 3100 B.C., the two kingdoms of Upper and Lower Egypt were united by a king called Menes.

Under later kings, called Pharaohs, the Egyptians developed one of the world's greatest ancient civilisations which lasted for over 3000 years. As well as constructing dams and canals to control the Nile and irrigate the land, they built great cities and enormous temples. But their most spectacular constructions were the massive pyramids. They were built as tombs for the early Pharaohs during the period known as the Old Kingdom (c. 2700-2200 B.C.).

It was later, during the Middle Kingdom (c. 2100-1750 B.C.) that Egypt probably first controlled Palestine and Syria. But c. 1750 B.C., Egypt itself was invaded and conquered by Semitic people from the east whom the Egyptians called the Hyksos, 'Rulers of foreign lands'. They made their capital at Avaris (Biblical Rameses) in the Nile Delta. This is one of the reasons which leads many Biblical scholars to place the story of Joseph's rise to power in Egypt during the Hyksos period. For it is evident from the account in Genesis that the Egyptian capital at this time was in the Delta area (Gen. 46.28 to 47.26).

But by about 1550 B.C., the Egyptians had managed to drive out the hated Hyksos. Egypt was then reunited under the Pharaohs of the New Kingdom (c. 1550-1080 B.C.). During this time Egypt became a major world power, and her empire stretched from the Nile to the Euphrates.

Meanwhile, the people living in the mountainous regions to the north and east of the Fertile Crescent were forming powerful new kingdoms. They were non-Semitic Indo-Aryan races who also invaded the Fertile Crescent. Among them were the Hurrians (the Horites of the Old Testament), who founded the kingdom of Mitanni about 1500 B.C., in the northern part of the Fertile Crescent, and the Hittites from Asia Minor. They were in constant conflict with each other – and Egypt. This meant that Palestine, owing to its strategic importance, was a continual battleground even before the Israelite conquest.

Bible Lands: Relief

Hungary

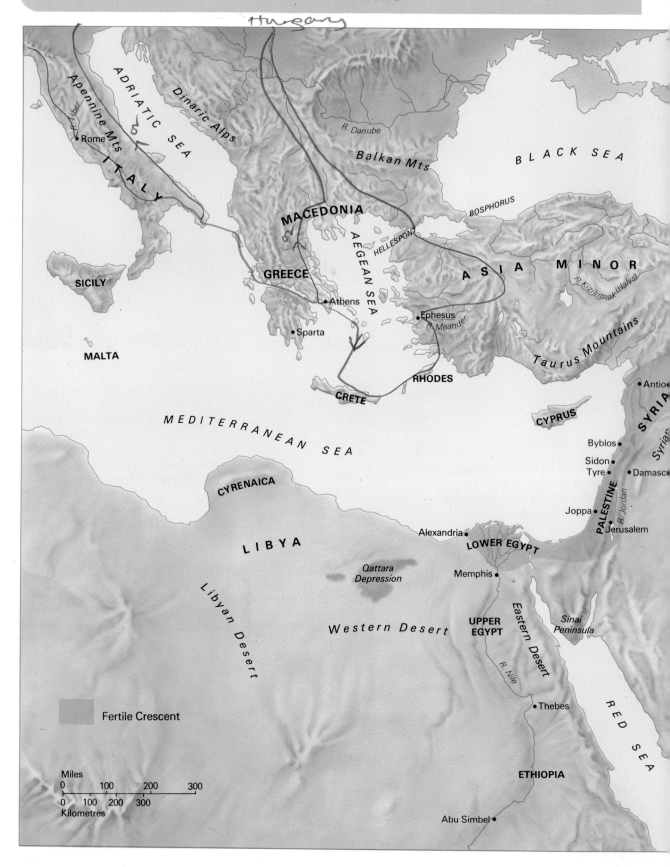

Apennine Mts
R. Tiber
Rome
ITALY
ADRIATIC SEA
Dinaric Alps
R. Danube
Balkan Mts
BLACK SEA
MACEDONIA
BOSPHORUS
HELLESPONT
AEGEAN SEA
ASIA MINOR
R. Kızılırmak (Halys)
GREECE
Athens
Ephesus
R. Meander
Taurus Mountains
Sparta
SICILY
RHODES
MALTA
CRETE
CYPRUS
Antio
SYRIA
MEDITERRANEAN SEA
Byblos
Sidon
Syrian
Tyre
Damasc
CYRENAICA
Joppa
PALESTINE
R. Jordan
Alexandria
Jerusalem
LOWER EGYPT
LIBYA
Qattara
Depression
Memphis
Western Desert
UPPER
EGYPT
Eastern Desert
Sinai
Peninsula
Libyan Desert
R. Nile
RED SEA
Thebes

Fertile Crescent

Miles
0   100   200   300
0 100 200 300
Kilometres

ETHIOPIA

Abu Simbel

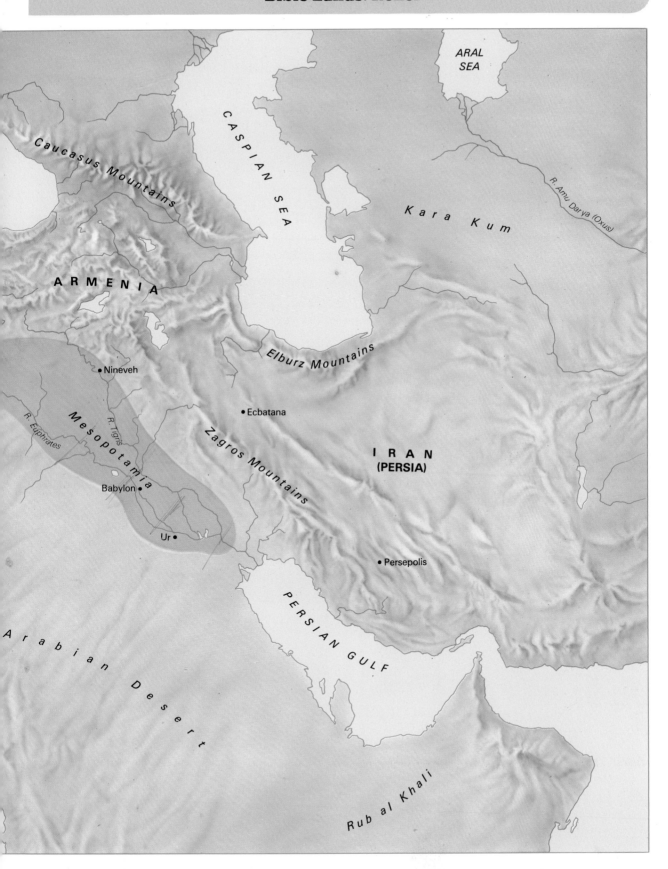

ARAL
SEA

C A S P I A N   S E A

Caucasus Mountains

K a r a   K u m

R. Amu Darya (Oxus)

A R M E N I A

Elburz Mountains

• Nineveh

• Ecbatana

R. Tigris

Mesopotamia

R. Euphrates

Zagros Mountains

I R A N
(PERSIA)

Babylon •

Ur •

• Persepolis

P E R S I A N   G U L F

A r a b i a n   D e s e r t

Rub al Khali

The lowest level of the vast Ziggurat at Ur, Iraq. It covers an area of 62.5 by 43 metres.

The map overleaf shows the main journeys of the Hebrew Patriarchs – Abraham, Isaac and Jacob – as recorded in Genesis 11.31 to 46.27. These chapters tell us how God established a special relationship with these people and their descendants.

About the year 2000 B.C., God chose Abraham, 'a man of faith', to be the father and founder of the Hebrew race. The story begins when Terah, Abraham's father, migrated with his family from Ur in the Plain of Mesopotamia to Haran in the north. God then called Abraham to leave Haran, and go to the land of Canaan, modern Israel. So Abraham went. At the same time, God made a promise to him. Although Abraham and his wife, Sarah, were both old and childless, God said to him, 'I will make of you a great nation, and I will bless you and make your name great so that you will be a blessing.' (Gen. 12.2.)

God's promise began to be fulfilled when Abraham was settled in Canaan at Mamre, near Hebron, and unexpectedly became the father of two sons – Ishmael and Isaac. Ishmael was 'the child of the flesh', as he was the son of Sarah's maid Hagar, and became the father of the Arabs. Isaac, on the other hand, was 'the child of promise', born to Sarah, Abraham's wife, according to God's promise (Gen. 17.19-21). It was through Isaac that the Hebrew line of descent was continued.

Isaac, who married Rebekah, also had two sons – Esau and Jacob. But it was Jacob who, by depriving Esau of his birthright and deceitfully obtaining his father's blessing, became the third Hebrew Patriarch whilst Esau became the father of the Edomites.

Ur.Excavation of a house associated with Abraham

Temple of Baal at Shechem

Abraham's well, Beer-sheba

Rachel's Tomb, Bethlehem

After deceiving his father, Jacob left Canaan and went to Haran in Mesopotamia where he worked for his uncle, Laban, for some years and also married Laban's two daughters – Leah and Rachel. By the time he returned to Canaan, Jacob had twelve sons whose descendants became the twelve tribes of Israel.

Jacob's favourite son, Joseph, was sold as a slave by his jealous brothers, and taken to Egypt where he was eventually imprisoned. In prison, Joseph interpreted the dreams of two other prisoners who were servants of the Pharaoh of Egypt. Later, Pharaoh himself had two dreams which no one could interpret. So he sent for Joseph, who explained that his dreams meant there would be seven years of great plenty in Egypt followed by seven years of severe famine. Joseph also advised Pharaoh to appoint a wise man to store grain during the seven plentiful years in preparation for the famine. The result was that Pharaoh appointed Joseph to organise the storage of grain, and made him governor of Egypt.

During the famine, which affected Canaan as well as Egypt, Jacob sent his eleven other sons to Egypt to buy grain. Eventually, when Joseph had made himself known to his brothers, Jacob and his family migrated from Canaan to Egypt where they prospered and multiplied. They became so numerous and strong that a later Pharaoh – possibly Rameses II (1290-1224 B.C.) – made them slaves (Ex. 1.8-11).

Mosque at Hebron where the Patriarchs are buried

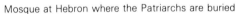

Troy

HITTITE EMPIRE

Carchemis[

Hal[
(Ale[

Ebla

Hamath

CYPRUS

MEDITERRANEAN SEA

Damascus

CANAAN

Hazor

R. Jordan

Shechem
Succoth

Bethel
Jerusalem

Hebron

Beer-sheba

Avaris

LOWER EGYPT

LIBYA

On (Heliopolis)

Memphis
(Noph)

R. Nile

SINAI

BLACK

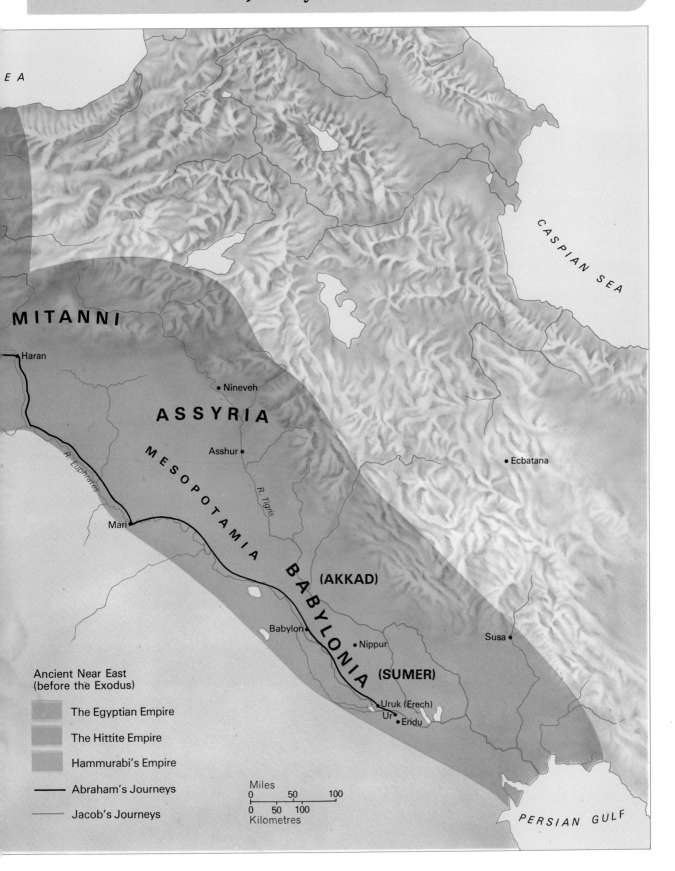

S E A

CASPIAN SEA

MITANNI

Haran

• Nineveh

ASSYRIA

Asshur •

R. Euphrates

M E S O P O T A M I A

R. Tigris

• Ecbatana

Mari •

B A B Y L O N I A

(AKKAD)

Babylon •

• Nippur

Susa •

(SUMER)

Uruk (Erech) •

Ur • • Eridu

Ancient Near East
(before the Exodus)

The Egyptian Empire

The Hittite Empire

Hammurabi's Empire

Abraham's Journeys

Jacob's Journeys

Miles
0   50   100

0   50   100
Kilometres

PERSIAN GULF

Sphinx and Cheop's pyramid at Giza, Egypt

When the Hebrews had been in Egypt for about 400 years, God called Moses to free them from their slavery and lead them back to the Promised Land of Canaan (Ex. 3). Eventually, after a series of plagues in Egypt, they miraculously escaped from the Egyptians by crossing the Sea of Reeds (or Red Sea?) on dry land into the Sinai desert (Ex. 14). This great event in the history of the Hebrews is known as the Exodus, and possibly took place during the reign of the Pharaoh Merneptah (1224-1216 B.C.). But it was not until forty years later, according to the Biblical accounts, that the Hebrews entered the Promised Land. During these years they were 'wandering in the wilderness'.

The exact route which Moses and the Hebrews took from Egypt to Canaan is uncertain because the Biblical accounts are confusing, and many of the places which they mention have not yet been identified. But the traditional route is shown on the map overleaf. This places the crossing of the sea at the southern end of Lake Menzaleh. After entering the wilderness of the Sinai desert, it is thought that Moses decided to take an indirect, southerly, route to Canaan in order to avoid a number of Egyptian fortresses which guarded the direct, easterly, route known as 'The Way to the Land of the Philistines'.

A southerly route is also based on the ancient tradition that Mount Sinai – where Moses received the Law from God (Ex. 19 to 25.) – is the present day Jebel Musa (the mountain of Moses) in the south of the Sinai peninsula. Certainly, Christian hermits were living on this mountain as early as the 4th century A.D., and in the 6th century A.D., the emperor Justinian built the famous monastery of St. Catherine here, which is still occupied by Christian monks.

Statue of Rameses II at Karnak, Egypt

St. Catherine's Monastery, Mount Sinai

From Mount Sinai the Hebrews travelled in a north-easterly direction through the wilderness of the Sinai desert to the oasis of Kadesh-barnea, a site which has been identified south of the Negeb desert. Moses evidently planned to invade Canaan from Kadesh-barnea because it was from here that he sent twelve men to spy out the land.

The spies discovered that the land was indeed 'flowing with milk and honey', but occupied by people living in strong, fortified cities (Num. 13 to 14). When the Hebrews heard their discouraging report, they were too frightened to enter Canaan, and remained at Kadesh-barnea for some time. Moses then decided to invade Canaan from the east. But the king of Edom refused to give him permission to travel north along the King's Highway – the main trade route from Ezion-geber to Damascus (Num. 20.14-21).

Once again the Hebrews were forced to resume their wanderings. They went from Kadesh-barnea to Mount Hor, where Aaron died, and then turned south to Ezion-geber before taking a route north to avoid passing through Edom and Moab. But when Sihon, king of the Amorites, refused to allow them to travel through his kingdom a battle was fought at Jahaz. Sihon was killed and his territory captured. The Hebrews then moved further north along the King's Highway to Bashan where they fought and defeated the giant king Og at the battle of Edrei (Deut. 2.26 to 3.11).

The result of these victories was that the Hebrews occupied the east bank of the River Jordan – from Mount Hermon in the north to the River Arnon in the south. They were now in a position to invade Canaan itself, and Moses gathered his people together on the plains of Moab in preparation for the advance. But Moses was denied the joy of leading them into Canaan himself. After viewing the Promised Land from the summit of Mount Nebo and appointing Joshua his successor, he died (Deut. 34.1-7).

Mount Hor — traditional burial place of Aaron (Jordan)

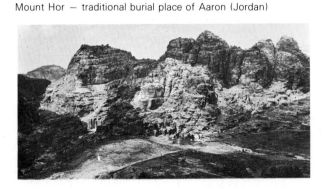

Wadi Musa (The Fountain of Moses) Jordan

MEDITERRANEAN SEA

Lake Menzaleh

Rameses
(Avaris)
Baal-zephon
Zilu

Way to the land o

G O S H E N
Succoth
Pithom

W i l d e r n e s s

Bitter Lakes

L I B Y A

E
G
Y
P
T

Heliopolis (On)

Way to Arabi

Memphis
(Noph)

Lake Moeris

Marah

Elim

Heracleopolis

R. Nile

Dophka

G u l f   o f   S u e z

Akhetaton

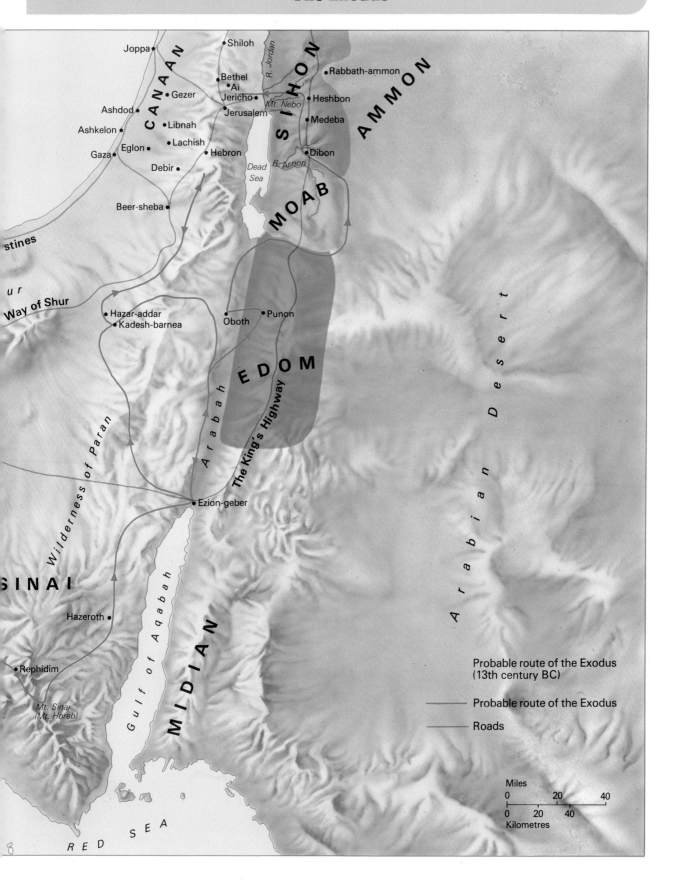

Joppa

CANAAN

Shiloh

Bethel
Ai
Gezer
Jericho
Jerusalem
Ashdod
Libnah
Ashkelon
Lachish
Eglon
Gaza
Hebron
Debir

Beer-sheba

stines

ur

Way of Shur

Hazar-addar
Kadesh-barnea

Oboth
Punon

R. Jordan
SIHON
Rabbath-ammon
Heshbon
Mt. Nebo
Medeba
AMMON
Dibon
Dead
Sea
R. Arnon
MOAB

EDOM

Arabah

The King's Highway

Arabian Desert

Wilderness of Paran

SINAI

Hazeroth

Rephidim

Mt. Sinai
(Mt. Horeb)

Ezion-geber

Gulf of Aqabah

MIDIAN

RED   SEA

Probable route of the Exodus
(13th century BC)

——— Probable route of the Exodus

——— Roads

Miles
0   20   40

0   20   40
Kilometres

After the death of Moses, God called Joshua to lead the Hebrews, or Israelites, into Canaan (Josh. 1.1-2). He sent two men to spy out Jericho, and then led the people of Israel from Moab across the river Jordan – when its waters were cut off between Adam and the Dead Sea – to Gilgal. After destroying Jericho and Ai, and defeating an alliance of five kings at Gibeon, Joshua conquered the south of the country. After defeating another alliance of kings in a battle at the Waters of Merom, he also destroyed the strategic city of Hazor and conquered the north of the country.

Joshua, however, did not succeed in conquering the entire land of Canaan, which was occupied not only by Canaanites but also by people of other races, including the Philistines. The Canaanites, for example, continued

River Jordan

Petra, High place of Sacrifice (Jordan)

Jordan. Their leaders at this time were popular hero-deliverers called 'Judges' whose dramatic exploits are recorded in the Book of Judges.

Ehud, for example, defeated the Moabites (Judg. 3.12-30) and Deborah with her army commander, Barak, won a decisive victory over the Canaanites (Judg. 4 to 5). Gideon, similarly, attacked and defeated the Midianites (Judg. 6.1 to 8.28) and Jephthah slaughtered the Ammonites (Judg. 10.17-33). But it was the Philistines who became the Israelites' most formidable foe. Their strength became apparent during the time of Samson, the last of the 'Judges', whose many daring attacks against them ended in his death (Judg. 13 to 16).

Remains of Old Testament Jericho

to occupy many important cities, and the Philistines remained in control of their five key cities – Gaza, Ashdod, Ashkelon, Gath and Ekron (Josh. 13.1-7). Nevertheless, Joshua divided up the land amongst the tribes. Reuben, Gad and half the tribe of Manasseh had already been allotted the occupied land on the east bank of the Jordan (Josh. 14.3-4). Now, in Canaan, lots were cast at Gilgal and Shiloh for the division of the land amongst the other nine tribes and half the tribe of Manasseh, as shown on the map (Josh. 14.6 to 19.48). Six cities of refuge were appointed (Josh. 20) and forty-eight cities were given to the Levites (Josh. 21.1-42). Finally, before he died, Joshua gathered all the tribes at Shechem and, like Moses at Mount Sinai, he made a covenant – or agreement – with his people, who promised to be faithful in serving God (Josh. 24).

After the death of Joshua the Israelites not only continued to fight their enemies in Canaan, but also fought the people who attacked them from the east bank of the

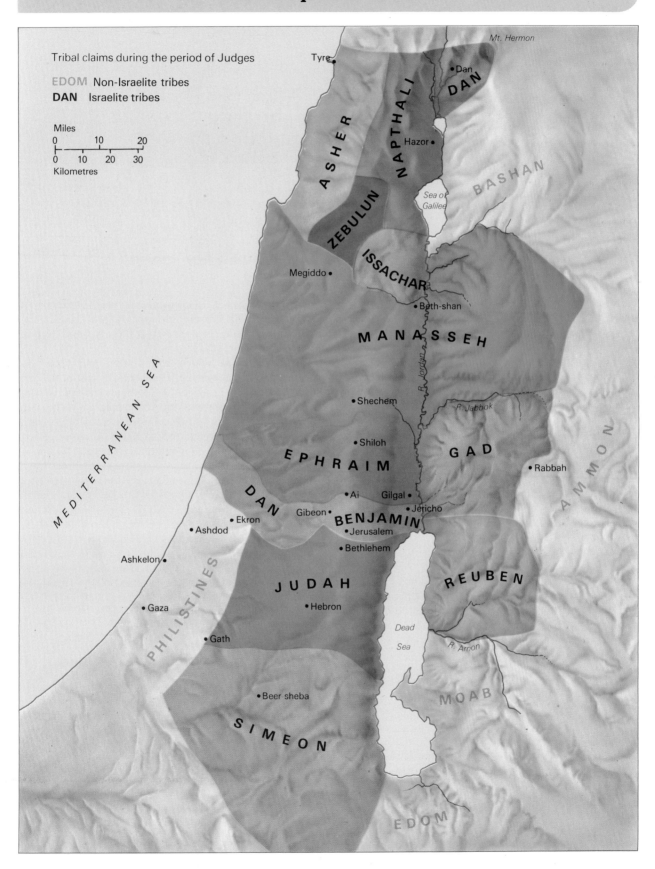

Tribal claims during the period of Judges

EDOM Non-Israelite tribes
DAN Israelite tribes

Miles
0   10   20
0   10   20   30
Kilometres

Mt. Hermon

Tyre

Dan

DAN

NAPTHALI

Hazor

BASHAN

ASHER

ZEBULUN

Sea of Galilee

ISSACHAR

Megiddo

Beth-shan

MANASSEH

R. Jordan

MEDITERRANEAN SEA

Shechem

R. Jabbok

Shiloh

EPHRAIM

GAD

Rabbah

DAN

Ai

Gilgal

AMMON

Gibeon

Jericho

Ekron

BENJAMIN

Ashdod

Jerusalem

Bethlehem

Ashkelon

PHILISTINES

REUBEN

JUDAH

Gaza

Hebron

Gath

Dead Sea

R. Arnon

Beer sheba

MOAB

SIMEON

EDOM

Stone carving of the
Ark of the Covenant,
Capernaum

Towards the end of the period of the Judges (c. 1200-1020 B.C.) the Israelites were faced with a crisis. Their occupation of Canaan was threatened by the growing power of the Philistines, who had already extended their territory eastwards.

During the time of Samuel, the Philistines defeated the Israelites in a battle at Eben-ezer. The Israelites, in despair, then sent to the sanctuary at Shiloh for the sacred Ark of the Covenant in the hope that it would enable them to defeat the Philistines. But the Israelites were again defeated in a second major battle at Eben-ezer where the Philistines slaughtered them in their thousands, and also captured the sacred Ark (1 Sam. 4.1-11). However, when they were suddenly afflicted with a plague, the Philistines thought the Ark was responsible and returned it to the Israelites at Beth-she-mesh. From here, the Israelites took the Ark to Kiriath-jearim where it remained for twenty years (1 Sam. 5.1 to 7.3).

After their great victory, the Philistines occupied much of Canaan. The Israelites then asked Samuel to appoint a king to rule over them, and lead them in their fight against their enemies (1 Sam. 8.4-22). The result was that Saul – a man from the tribe of Benjamin renowned for his bravery and great height – became the first Israelite king in about 1020 B.C. (1 Sam. 10.1 to 11.15).

The first battle which Saul fought and won was against the Ammonites at Jabesh-gilead, east of the Jordan (1 Sam. 11.1-13). Then, helped by Jonathan his son, he successfully attacked the Philistines at Michmash, north of Jerusalem, which enabled him to drive them out of the central hill country (1 Sam. 14.1-46).

Although the Philistines continued to attack the Israelites throughout Saul's reign, he managed to hold them in check, and maintained his control over much of Canaan, as the map shows, until the death of Samuel. Then, the Philistines gathered their forces at Aphek and advanced northwards to the Plain of Esdraelon where a major battle was fought. The Philistines inflicted a crushing defeat on the Israelites, and Saul committed suicide on nearby Mount Gilboa after three of his sons, including Jonathan, had been killed. Once again the triumphant Philistines controlled much of Canaan, and also occupied land east of the Jordan.

Tell at Beth-shan

Plain of Esdraelon

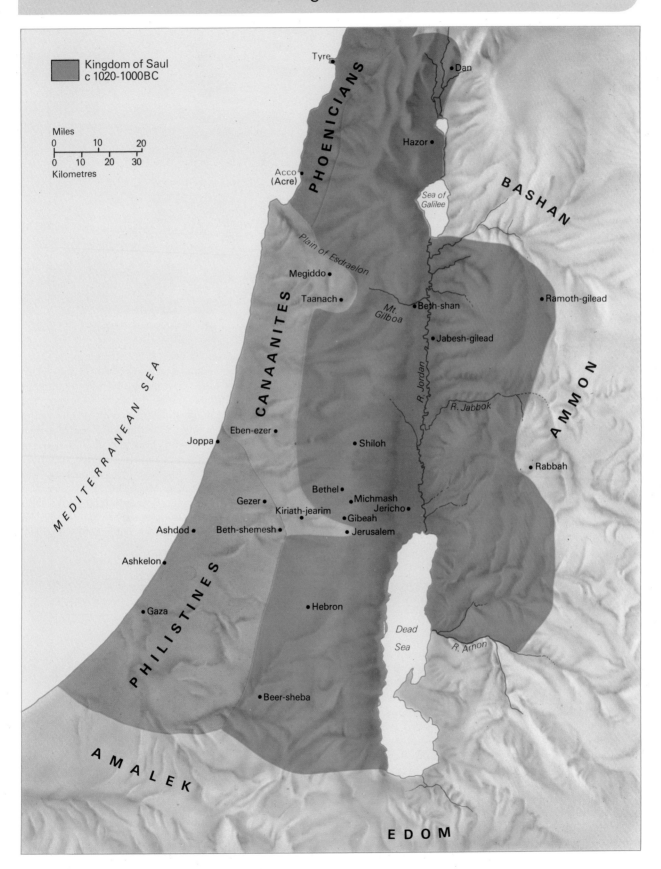

Kingdom of Saul
c 1020-1000BC

Miles
0   10   20
0 10 20 30
Kilometres

Tyre
Dan
PHOENICIANS
Hazor
BASHAN
Acco
(Acre)
Sea of
Galilee
Plain of Esdraelon
Megiddo
Ramoth-gilead
Taanach
Mt.
Gilboa
Beth-shan
Jabesh-gilead
R. Jordan
CANAANITES
R. Jabbok
AMMON
MEDITERRANEAN SEA
Eben-ezer
Shiloh
Joppa
Rabbah
Bethel
Gezer
Michmash
Jericho
Kiriath-jearim
Gibeah
Ashdod
Beth-shemesh
Jerusalem
Ashkelon
PHILISTINES
Hebron
Dead
Sea
R. Arnon
Gaza
Beer-sheba
AMALEK
EDOM

After the death of Saul, Ishbosheth, one of his sons, became king of the northern tribes of Israel at Mahanaim, east of the Jordan (2 Sam. 2.8-10). But David, who rose to prominence during Saul's reign, was proclaimed king of the southern tribe of Judah at Hebron (2 Sam. 2.1-4). However, about 1000 B.C., after the murder of Ishbosheth, David became king of all Israel (2 Sam. 4.5 to 5.5) and a new era in the history of the Israelites began. For, under David, the northern tribes of Israel and the southern tribe of Judah first became a nation, and formed a strong united kingdom.

Meanwhile, after reigning in Hebron for seven years, David captured the strategic Jebusite city of Jerusalem, and made it his new capital (2 Sam. 5.6-8). He also made Jerusalem the religious, as well as the political, capital of his kingdom by bringing the sacred Ark from Kiriath-jearim to the city (2 Sam. 6). So Jerusalem, the city of David, also became the Holy City of God.

Stone terraces dating from David's time, Jerusalem

A view of Hebron

David's swift rise to power, however, soon alarmed the Philistines, who gathered a great army near Jerusalem to overthrow him. But David defeated them so decisively in two major battles that their power was broken, and they never again became a serious threat to Israel (2 Sam. 5.17-25). He then attacked and conquered the nations east of the Jordan, and extended his kingdom from the river Euphrates to the borders of Egypt (2 Sam. 8.3). But towards the end of his reign two unsuccessful attempts were made to topple David from his throne (2 Sam. 15.1-22). Then, shortly before he died, Adonijah, David's oldest surviving son, tried to obtain the throne. But David appointed Solomon, his son by Bathsheba, to succeed him as king (1 Kings 1.).

Solomon's reign (c. 961-922 B.C.) was a time of peace and prosperity for Israel, and renowned for the splendour and glory of his achievements. He did not attempt to extend the empire which he had inherited, but strengthened it by making alliances with neighbouring countries, and engaging in world-wide trade, which greatly increased his wealth. Solomon also carried out a vast building programme, which included the magnificent First Temple in Jerusalem, royal palaces, and the fortified cities of Hazor, Megiddo, and Gezer. But towards the end of his reign Solomon forsook the faith of his forefathers, and his oppressive rule resulted in discontent and revolt amongst his subjects (1 Kings 11).

Excavations at Megiddo

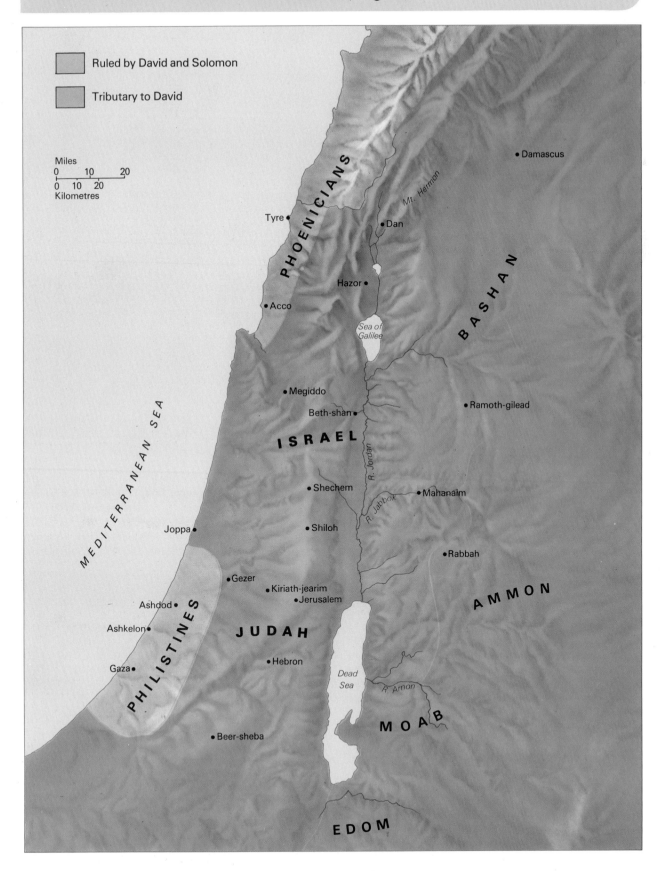

Ruled by David and Solomon

Tributary to David

Miles
0   10   20
0 10 20
Kilometres

PHOENICIANS

BASHAN

• Damascus

Mt. Hermon

Tyre •

• Dan

Hazor •

• Acco

Sea of
Galilee

• Megiddo

Beth-shan •

• Ramoth-gilead

ISRAEL

R. Jordan

MEDITERRANEAN SEA

• Shechem

• Mahanaim

R. Jabbok

• Shiloh

Joppa •

• Rabbah

• Gezer

• Kiriath-jearim

Ashdod •

• Jerusalem

AMMON

Ashkelon •

JUDAH

Gaza •

PHILISTINES

• Hebron

Dead
Sea

R. Arnon

• Beer-sheba

MOAB

EDOM

When Solomon died, about 922 B.C., the tension and discontent amongst the people led to the permanent division of his kingdom. The ten northern tribes broke away from the Dynasty of David to form the kingdom of Israel. Their first king was Jeroboam, a man from the tribe of Ephraim who had previously led an unsuccessful revolt against Solomon (1 Kings 11.26-40). He made his capital at Shechem, which was later moved to Tirzah and then to Samaria (1 Kings 16.24). The two southern tribes of Judah and Benjamin, however, remained faithful to the Dynasty of David. They formed the kingdom of Judah under King Rehoboam, Solomon's son, whose capital was at Jerusalem (1 Kings 14.21).

The political separation of the two kingdoms was also accompanied by a religious division. For, as Solomon's temple at Jerusalem was now situated in Judah, Jeroboam built two rival temples in Israel – at Dan in the north and Bethel in the south. In each temple he set up a golden statue of a bull-calf (1 Kings 12.25-33).

Statue of Elijah at Muhraqa on Mount Carmel

Excavations at Dan

Jeroboam is strongly condemned in the Bible because 'he caused Israel to sin' by promoting and encouraging idolatry amongst the people. But he was not the only king during the period of the Divided Kingdom to lead his people astray from the true worship of Yahweh. The prophet Elijah, for example, opposed Ahab of Israel and his wife Jezebel because they promoted the worship of the pagan god Baal (1 Kings 18). Later prophets – such as Amos and Hosea in Israel, and Isaiah and Jeremiah in Judah – condemned pagan worship too, and tried to lead the people back to the true worship of Yahweh. They also condemned the social evils in their countries, and often opposed the political policies of their kings.

During the period of their separation, the two kingdoms were frequently at war with each other, which made them an easy prey to attacks from neighbouring countries. Both kingdoms, for example, fought the Egyptians, Moabites and Syrians, and Judah also fought the Philistines, Ammonites and Edomites. But in the middle of the 8th century B.C., they faced their most powerful enemy – the mighty empire of Assyria. In 722 B.C., the Assyrians finally conquered and occupied Israel, which ended the period of the Divided Kingdom.

Tower of the West Gate, Samaria

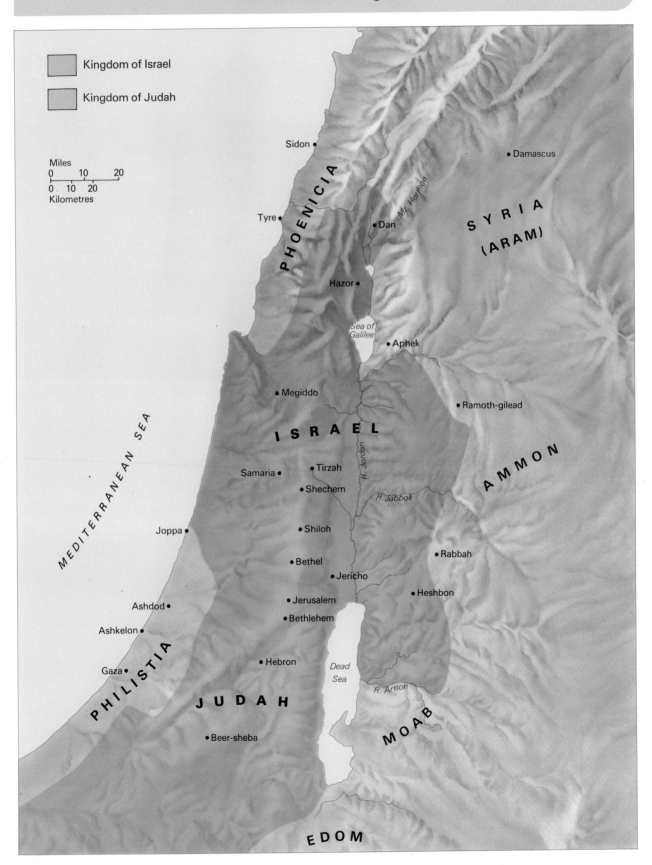

Kingdom of Israel

Kingdom of Judah

Miles
0   10   20
0   10   20
Kilometres

Sidon •

• Damascus

PHOENICIA

Mt. Hermon

Tyre •

• Dan

S Y R I A
(ARAM)

Hazor •

Sea of Galilee

• Aphek

MEDITERRANEAN SEA

• Megiddo

I S R A E L

R. Jordan

Samaria •   • Tirzah

• Shechem

R. Jabbok

A M M O N

Joppa •

• Shiloh

• Bethel

• Rabbah

• Jericho

Ashdod •

• Jerusalem

• Heshbon

• Bethlehem

Ashkelon •

PHILISTIA

Gaza •

• Hebron

Dead Sea

J U D A H

R. Arnon

M O A B

• Beer-sheba

E D O M

Reconstructed wall and gate, Nineveh (Iraq)

Boat on the River Euphrates

Site of Asshur on the River Tigris

It was during the period of the Divided Kingdom that the Assyrians established their great empire, which eventually stretched from Mesopotamia to Egypt.

After extending their frontiers in the east, the Assyrian kings turned their armies against the west, which brought Israel and Judah on to the stage of world history. They first conquered Syria and received tribute from Israel. Tiglath-pileser III (745-727 B.C.) then occupied a large part of Israel, but Hoshea was allowed to rule the remaining territory from Samaria, the capital, as a vassal king. Hoshea, however, rebelled against Assyria during the reign of Shalmaneser V (727-722 B.C.), who invaded his territory and besieged Samaria. The siege lasted three years, and Samaria finally fell in 722 B.C., during the reign of Sargon II (722-705 B.C.), bringing the Kingdom of Israel to an end. Sargon deported the people to Assyria, which is the last we hear of the 'lost ten tribes of Israel'. He then replaced them by foreign settlers, who were later known as 'Samaritans' (2 Kings 17.5 and 6.24).

Meanwhile, although Judah had been an Assyrian vassal-state since the time of Tiglath-pileser, she had escaped invasion. But when Hezekiah (715-687 B.C.) rebelled against Assyria, Sennacherib (705-681 B.C.) attacked Judah. While he was blockading Jerusalem, however, his army was stricken with a plague and Sennacherib suddenly withdrew to Nineveh, his capital. Jerusalem escaped destruction, and Judah survived. But her days were numbered. For, less than a century later, the Assyrian empire fell to the Babylonians, which sealed the fate of Judah.

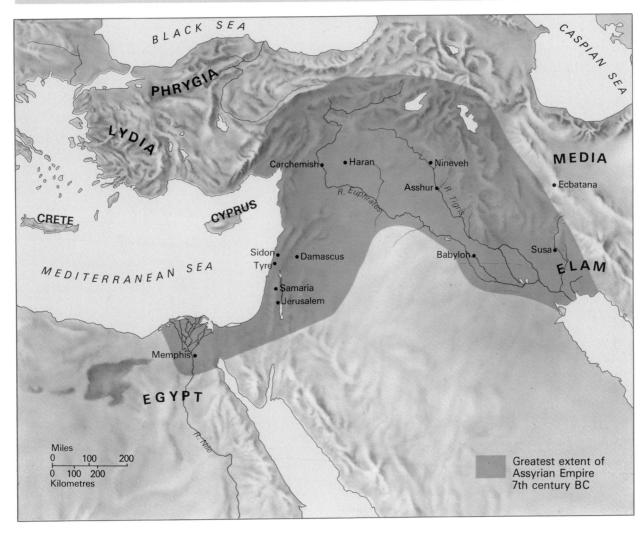

Remains of Ziggurat, Nimrud (Iraq)

Relief of Assurnasirpal, Nimrud

Excavations and reconstructed E-Makh Temple at Babylon, Iraq

Assyria reached the peak of her power during the reign of Ashurbanipal (668-630 B.C.). But, after his death, her great empire soon fell to the Medes and Babylonians, who destroyed Nineveh, the capital, in 612 B.C., and finally defeated the Assyrians at Haran in 609 B.C.

Meanwhile, Josiah of Judah (640-609 B.C.) had tried to prevent Pharaoh Neco of Egypt from going to the aid of the Assyrians. But Neco defeated and killed Josiah at Megiddo (2 Kings 23.29-30). He occupied Syria and Palestine for a short while before his army was annihilated by the Babylonians under Nebuchadnezzar (605-562 B.C.) at Carchemish in 605 B.C. Judah then became a Babylonian vassal state. But it was not long before

Nebuchadnezzar had to put down a revolt. In 597 B.C. he attacked Jerusalem, deported a large number of people to Babylon, and appointed Zedekiah as a vassal king (2 Kings 24). But he, too, rebelled – in spite of warnings from the prophet Jeremiah. Once again, Nebuchadnezzar attacked Judah. In 587 B.C., he destroyed the entire city of Jerusalem, including Solomon's Temple, and once more deported many people to Babylon. Among them was Zedekiah, who was replaced by a governor – Gedaliah. But he was soon murdered. Then, most of the remaining people – accompanied by Jeremiah – fled to Egypt. This was the end of the Kingdom of Judah (2 Kings 25).

Remains of the Ishtar Gate, Babylon

Reconstruction of the Ishtar Gate, Babylon

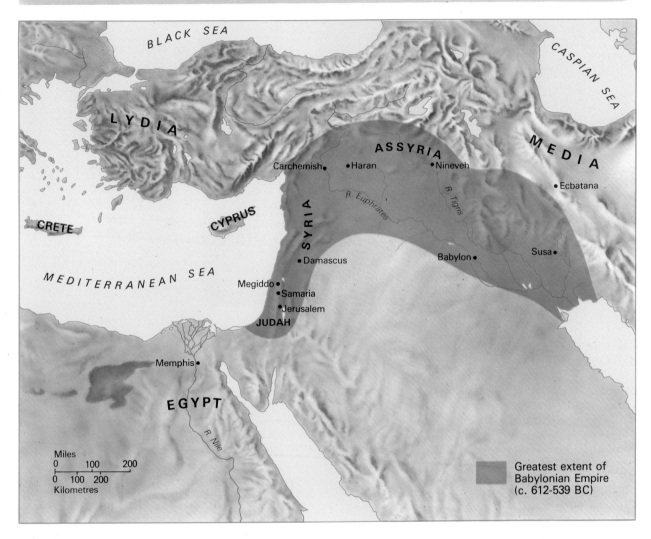

Nebuchadnezzar II's Palace, Babylon, Iraq

The Lion of Babylon dates from Nebuchadnezzar's reign

Tomb of Cyrus at Pasargadae, Iran

When the people of Judah were deported to Babylon, the story of the Jews begins. For, unlike the people of Israel, the people of Judah retained their national identity and religion during their exile. Much of the Old Testament was also written down at this time.

The Jews remained in exile until the Babylonian empire was conquered by Cyrus, the founder of the vast Persian empire which, as the map shows, eventually stretched from India to Macedonia. Cyrus was hailed as 'The Lord's Anointed' (Isa. 45.1), and after capturing Babylon in 539 B.C., he gave the Jews permission to return to Judah and rebuild the Temple in Jerusalem. Many, but not all the Jews, returned to Judah. But the rebuilding of the Temple was not completed until 515 B.C., during the time of the prophets Haggai and Zechariah.

Later, during the fifth century B.C., Ezra, a priest, returned from Babylon with another group of exiles, and reorganised the religious life of the Jews (Ezra 7.1 to 10.17). About the same time, the walls of Jerusalem were rebuilt by Nehemiah, the Jewish governor (Neh. 2 to 7). He also carried out a number of social reforms (Neh. 13). Little is known of the history of the Jews during the rest of the Persian period, which ended when Alexander the Great of Macedon conquered the Persian empire in 333 B.C.

Gate of Xerxes in Persepolis, Iran

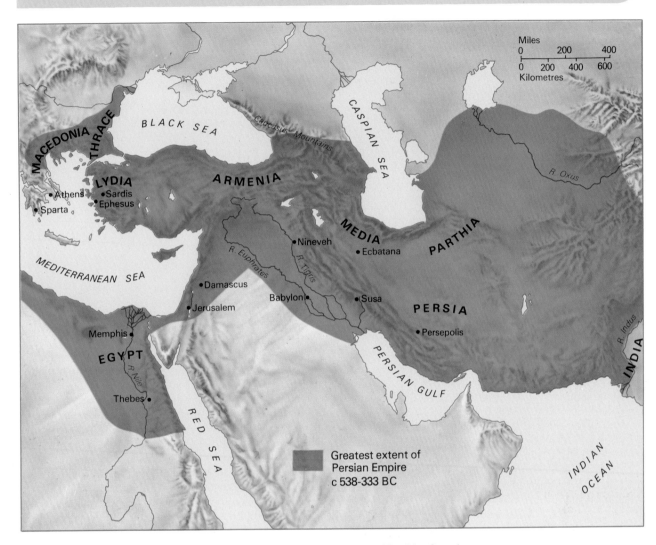

Rock Tomb of Xerxes at Naqsh-i-Rostem, Iran

Tomb of Daniel at Susa, Iran

Temple of Horus at Edfu, Egypt

During his campaigns against the Persians, Alexander the Great took control of Palestine. But when he died at Babylon in 323 B.C., his great empire was divided into three kingdoms under three rival dynasties. Macedonia was ruled by Antigonus, Egypt by the Ptolemies, and Syria by the Seleucids.

The Ptolemies of Egypt first controlled Palestine for over a century – until 198 B.C. Then, the Seleucid king of Syria, Antiochus III (223-187 B.C.) defeated Ptolemy V at Paneas, near the sources of the river Jordan, and added Palestine to his empire.

During their occupation of Palestine, the Seleucids tried to impose the Greek way of life and the Greek religion on the Jews – with some success (1 Macc. 1.11-15). But in 167 B.C., Antiochus IV – known as Antiochus Epiphanes (175-163 B.C.) – desecrated the Temple in Jerusalem, and prohibited the Jews from practising their religion (1 Macc. 1.20ff). This attack on the Jewish religion led to the Maccabean rebellion.

Under the Maccabees, the Jews not only regained their religious freedom, but also achieved a brief period of political independence – from 142 B.C. until the Romans conquered Palestine in 63 B.C. The Maccabean period, however, was marred by disputes between two Jewish religious sects which arose at this time – the Pharisees and Sadducees. A third sect – the Essenes – was also established during this period, and some of them almost certainly lived at Qumran on the shores of the Dead Sea. But little was known about the Essenes until 1947 when the famous Dead Sea Scrolls were first discovered hidden in caves near their monastery, which has now been excavated.

Maccabean Tomb, known as 'Absolom's Tomb', Jerusalem

Maccabean Tower, Jerusalem

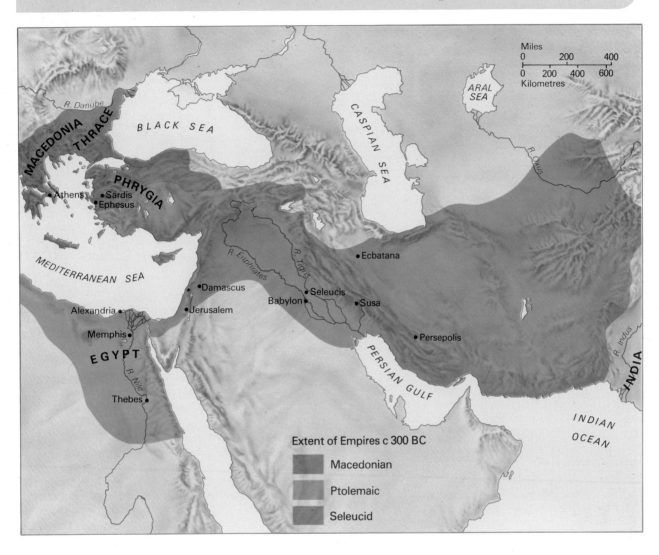

Miles
0   200   400
0   200   400   600
Kilometres

Extent of Empires c 300 BC

Macedonian

Ptolemaic

Seleucid

Mosaic of a lion hunt from Pella, Greece

Temple of Apollo at Corinth, Greece

The Forum of Rome, Italy

Statue of Augustus Caesar, Rome

Model of Herod's Temple, Jerusalem

Towards the end of the Maccabean period, the Romans began to extend their rule in the East. The Roman general Pompey took control of Syria, marched into Palestine, and captured Jerusalem in 63 B.C., after a three months' siege. The Jews in Palestine then lost their short-lived independence for over 2000 years – until 1948 when the present State of Israel was founded.

At first, the Roman governor of Syria controlled Palestine. Then, in 55 B.C., Julius Caesar made Antipater, an Idumean, procurator of Judea. When he was murdered in 43 B.C., the Roman Senate appointed Herod, one of Antipater's sons, king of the Jews. Known as Herod the Great, he ruled the Jews under the Romans for thirty-three years – from 37 B.C. to 4 B.C.

During his long reign, Herod undertook numerous building projects in Palestine and elsewhere. Remains of his magnificent cities, palaces, and fortresses can still be seen in the Holy Land today, for example, at Caesarea, Masada and Samaria, as well as in Jerusalem. Here, in an attempt to please the Jews, Herod began his most ambitious project – the rebuilding of the Temple. But Herod was a cruel and ruthless king, and the Jews hated him.

Nevertheless, it was during Herod's reign that God's preparation of the world for the birth of Jesus was completed. For, by this time, God had not only prepared the Jews for this great event. He had also prepared other nations so that the message of Christianity – the religion founded by Jesus – could be spread throughout the world. This was made possible because the Greeks had provided the world with a common language, and the Romans had established universal peace throughout their great empire, together with a remarkable network of roads. So, as St. Paul wrote later, 'When the time had

Roman aqueduct at Caesarea

The Egnatian Way near Kavalla (Neapolis), Greece

fully come, God sent forth his Son, born of woman . . .' (Gal. 4.4).

The Jewish woman whom God chose to be the mother of Jesus was the Virgin Mary (Lk. 1.26-38). Like Abraham, she was faithful to her divine calling, and Jesus was born at Bethlehem in Judea (Lk. 2.1-7). The exact date of his birth is not known. But it was about 6 B.C. – before the death of Herod in 4 B.C. (Matt. 2.13-16). (These dates are confusing because a monk in the 6th century, who fixed the Christian Calendar to begin in A.D. 1, made an error of about six years.)

When Herod died, his kingdom was divided between three of his surviving sons. Archelaus ruled over Judea, Samaria and Idumea; Herod Antipas over Galilee and Perea; and Philip over Iturea and Trachonitis (Lk. 3.1). But the Romans deposed Archelaus in A.D. 6, and placed his territory under the rule of procurators. One

of them was Pontius Pilate (A.D. 26-36), who condemned Jesus to death.

Later, Palestine was once more united for a short while under King Herod Agrippa I (A.D. 41-44), Herod the Great's grandson. But when he died, Roman procurators again ruled most of the country. Among them were Felix and Festus under whom St. Paul was a prisoner (Acts. 23 to 27).

When Florus (A.D. 64-66) was procurator, the First Jewish Revolt against the Romans broke out. This was crushed by Titus when he destroyed Jerusalem and burnt the Temple in A.D. 70 (cf. Lk. 19.41-44). In A.D. 135 a Second Jewish Revolt was also crushed. The emperor Hadrian (A.D. 117-138) then built a Roman city called Aelia Capitolina on the ruins of Jerusalem, which the Jews were forbidden to enter for two hundred years.

The fortress of Masada, used by Herod the Great

Mosaic of a Roman Chariot at Ostia, Italy

BRITANNIA

NORTH SEA

R. Rhine

GALLIA

Lugdunum •

ATLANTIC OCEAN

HISPANIA

• Massilia

ITALIA

• Tarraco

Rome •

• Valentia

Brundisium •

Gades •

MAURETANIA

Hippo Regius •

AFRICA

Syracuse •

Carthage •

M E D

• Leptis Magna

The Roman Empire
at the time of Jesus

Miles
0   200   400
0   200   400
Kilometres

BLACK SEA

CASPIAN SEA

R. Danube

THRACE

DONIA

Neapolis•

•Byzantium

ARMENIA

•Ancyra

ASIA

GALATIA

PARTHIA

Pergamum•

orinth

•Athens

•Ephesus

•Tarsus

R. Euphrates

•Antioch

R. Tigris

CYPRUS

SYRIA

CRETE

•Damascus

RANEAN SEA

JUDEA

•Cyrene

•Jerusalem

ENAICA

Alexandria•

EGYPT

Memphis•

R. Nile

RED SEA

Time chart for the Old Testament Period

B.C.	THE HEBREWS AND PALESTINE	THE EMPIRES
9000	Jericho occupied.	
3500		Mesopotamia: Kingdom of Sumer.
3100		Egypt: Upper and Lower Kingdoms united.
3000		Mesopotamia invaded by Semitic tribes.
2700–2200		Egypt: The Old Kingdom. Pyramids built.
2400		Syria: Canaanite Empire of Ebla.
2350–2200		Mesopotamia: Kingdom of Akkad.
2250		Syria: Ebla destroyed by Narum-Sin of Akkad.
2200		Mesopotamia invaded by Gutians.
2100–1750		Egypt: The Middle Kingdom.
2000		Mesopotamia invaded by Amorites.
2000–1750	Hebrew Patriarchs in Palestine.	
1890		Mesopotamia: Old Babylonian Empire.
1792		Hammurabi King of Babylon.
		Mari destroyed by Hammurabi.
1750		Egypt invaded by Hyksos.
		Joseph rises to power in Egypt
	Jacob and his family migrate to Egypt.	
1550		Egypt: Hyksos expelled.
1550–1080		Egypt: The New Kingdom.
1500		Mesopotamia invaded by the Horites.
		Kingdom of Mitanni.
1475–1200		Asia Minor: Hittite New Kingdom.
1400–1200		Syria: Canaanite City-state of Ugarit.
1290–1224	Hebrews in bondage in Egypt.	Rameses II Pharaoh of Egypt.
1224–1216	Exodus from Egypt.	Merneptah Pharaoh of Egypt.
	Palestine invaded by the Hebrews under Joshua.	
1200–1020	Period of the Judges.	
1190	Coastal plain of Palestine occupied by the Philistines.	
1050	Battle of Eben-ezer.	
	Philistines defeated Israelites.	
1020–1000	Saul king	
1000–961	David king. The United Kingdom.	
961–922	Solomon king.	

B.C.	JUDAH	ISRAEL	ASSYRIAN EMPIRE
922	Rehoboam	Jeroboam I	
883			Ashurnasirpal II
876		Omri	
873	Jehoshaphat		
861		Ahab	
859			Shalmaneser III
853			Battle of Qarqar
842		Jehu	
786		Jeroboam II	
783	Uzziah		
745			Tiglath-pileser III
732		Hoshea	
727			Shalmaneser V
722		Fall of Samaria and the end of the Kingdom of Israel	Sargon II

B.C.	THE HEBREWS AND PALESTINE	THE EMPIRES
	JUDAH	**ASSYRIAN EMPIRE**
715	Hezekiah	
705		Sennacherib
687	Manasseh	
668		Ashurbanipal
640	Josiah	
612		Fall of Nineveh
609		Fall of Haran
		BABYLONIAN EMPIRE
605	Jerusalem taken by Nebuchadnezzar. Many Jews exiled including Ezekiel.	Battle of Carchemish at which the Egyptians were defeated.
597	Zedekiah	
587	Fall of Jerusalem. Babylonian Exile.	
539		Fall of Babylon.
		PERSIAN EMPIRE
538	First return of Exiles.	Cyrus
520–515	Rebuilding of the Temple.	
522		Darius I
486		Xerxes I
465		Artaxerxes I
458	Return of Ezra.	
445	Arrival of Nehemiah. Rebuilding of Jerusalem's walls.	
333		**EMPIRE OF ALEXANDER THE GREAT**
323		**PTOLEMAIC AND SELEUCID EMPIRES**
323		Ptolemy I
312	Ptolemy I takes Palestine.	Seleucius king at Babylon. Antiochus III
223		
203		Ptolemy V
198	Antiochus III takes Palestine.	
175		Antiochus IV
167	Temple desecrated by Antiochus IV. Maccabean rebellion.	
164	Temple rededicated.	
142	The Maccabean Kingdom.	**ROMAN EMPIRE**
64		Pompey in Syria
63	Pompey takes Jerusalem.	
53–43	Antipater, Procurator of Judea.	
37	Herod the Great, King of Judea.	
27		Augustus Caesar

(*Dates are approximate*)

Part of the Jordan Valley from Jericho

In spite of its small size, Palestine has a very varied relief and climate. There are four main geographical regions.

1. *The Coastal Plain.* This includes the Plain of Acco, or Acre, to the north of Mount Carmel; the Plain of Sharon between Mount Carmel and Joppa; and the Plain of Philistia, south of Joppa.

2. *The Central Highlands.* These form the backbone of Palestine. The highlands of Galilee, however, are separated from the hill country of Samaria and Judea by the Plain of Esdraelon. The land where the Judean hills on the east descend steeply to the Jordan Valley is known as the Wilderness of Judea. On the west, between the hill country of Judea and the Plain of Philistia, lies the Shephelah, or Lowlands.

3. *The Jordan Valley.* This is part of a great rift valley which divides eastern from western Palestine. From its sources above Dan (329 metres above sea level), the River Jordan flows down to the Sea of Galilee (212 metres below sea level) and then to the Dead Sea (392 metres below sea level). The rift valley continues through the Arabah to the Red Sea and extends into East Africa.

4. *The Eastern Plateau.* This is divided by four rivers – the Yarmuk, Jabbok, Arnon and Zered. The height of the plateau, which is largely treeless but reasonably fertile, ranges from 600 to 1200 metres. The desert lies to the east.

Plain of Lebonah. The ancient frontier between Judea and Samaria ran along the foot of these hills.

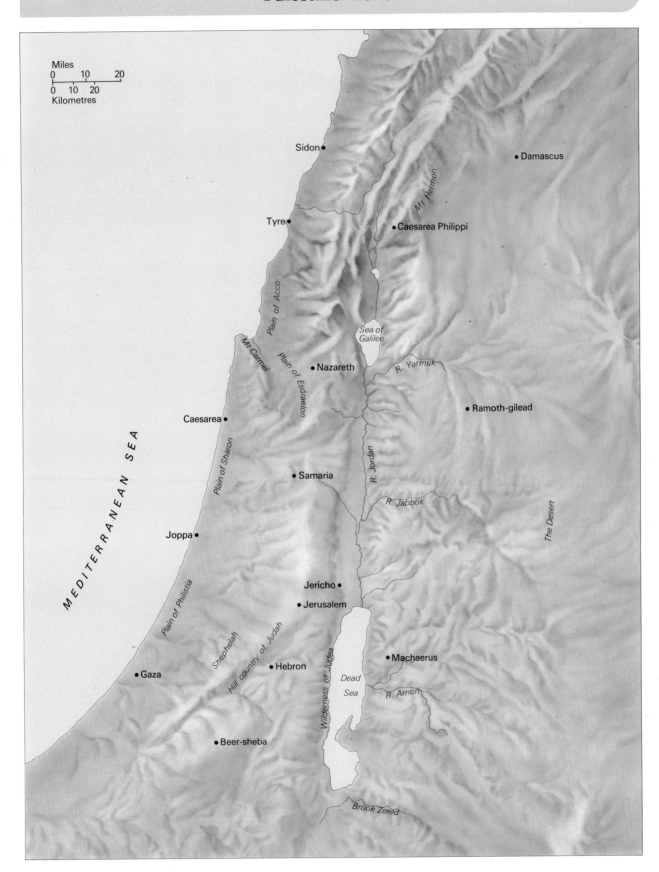

Miles
0 10 20
0 10 20
Kilometres

Sidon

Damascus

Mt Hermon

Tyre

Caesarea Philippi

Plain of Acco

Mt Carmel

Sea of Galilee

Plain of Esdraelon

Nazareth

R. Yarmuk

Caesarea

Ramoth-gilead

Plain of Sharon

R. Jordan

M E D I T E R R A N E A N   S E A

Samaria

R. Jabbok

The Desert

Joppa

Plain of Philistia

Jericho

Jerusalem

Shephelah

Hill country of Judah

Machaerus

Gaza

Hebron

Wilderness of Judea

Dead Sea

R. Arnon

Beer-sheba

Brook Zered

When Jesus was born, Palestine was part of the Roman Empire. But, as we have seen, it was governed by Herod the Great. When he died in 4 B.C., the land was divided into three main political areas, which were governed by three of Herod's sons.

Archelaus ruled over Judea, Samaria and Idumea from 4 B.C. to A.D. 6 when the emperor, Augustus, placed them under the control of Roman procurators until A.D. 41. Their capital was at Caesarea, a coastal city built by Herod the Great. But during the Jewish festival of the Passover, the procurators stayed in Jerusalem at the Praetorium – the Roman headquarters where troops were stationed. This accounts for Pontius Pilate's presence in Jerusalem at the Passover when the Jews handed Jesus over to him (Mk. 15).

Nazareth today

View of Bethlehem

Herod Antipas ruled over Galilee and Perea from 4 B.C. to A.D. 39. His first capital was at Sepphoris, four miles north of Nazareth, in Galilee. Later in his reign Antipas built a new capital on the western shore of the Sea of Galilee, which he named Tiberias in honour of the emperor. Jesus did not visit either of these non-Jewish cities. But he spent most of his life at Nazareth, and carried out much of his ministry in Galilee. This explains why Pilate sent Jesus to Herod Antipas during his trial (Lk. 23. 6-12). Antipas was also the King Herod responsible for beheading John the Baptist (Mk. 6. 14-30).

Philip ruled the area north-east of Galilee – Ituraea and Trachonitis – from 4 B.C. to A.D. 34. Like Herod Antipas, Philip also built a new city in honour of the emperor – Caesarea Philippi – which was his capital. Jesus visited this district before his Transfiguration (Mk. 8.27). He also visited another new city built by Philip – Bethsaida Julias, which is called Bethsaida in the Gospels (Mk. 6.45; 8.22).

South of Philip's territory was the Decapolis – a Greek word meaning 'Ten Cities'. In this region there was originally a league of ten independent Greek cities, which were protected by the Roman governor of Syria. The number of cities in the league, however, seems to have varied from time to time. Scythopolis, previously called Bethshan, was the most important, and the only one situated west of the Jordan. Among the others was Gerasa (known today as Jerash) and Philadelphia (now Amman, the capital of Jordan). During his ministry Jesus visited the Decapolis on at least two occasions. (Matt. 8 28; Mk. 7.31).

The Roman road from Jerusalem to Jericho

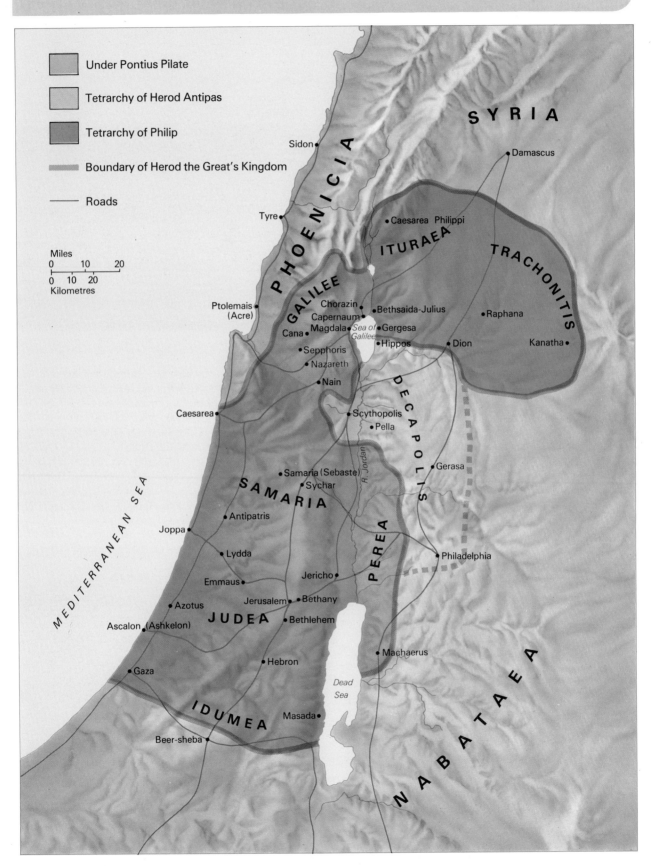

Legend:
- Under Pontius Pilate
- Tetrarchy of Herod Antipas
- Tetrarchy of Philip
- Boundary of Herod the Great's Kingdom
- Roads

Miles
0 10 20

Kilometres
0 10 20

SYRIA

PHOENICIA

ITURAEA

TRACHONITIS

GALILEE

DECAPOLIS

SAMARIA

PEREA

JUDEA

IDUMEA

NABATAEA

MEDITERRANEAN SEA

Dead Sea

Sea of Galilee

R. Jordan

Sidon

Damascus

Tyre

Caesarea Philippi

Ptolemais (Acre)

Chorazin

Bethsaida-Julius

Raphana

Capernaum

Cana

Magdala

Gergesa

Sepphoris

Hippos

Dion

Kanatha

Nazareth

Caesarea

Nain

Scythopolis

Pella

Samaria (Sebaste)

Sychar

Gerasa

Antipatris

Joppa

Lydda

Philadelphia

Emmaus

Jericho

Azotus

Jerusalem

Bethany

Ascalon (Ashkelon)

Bethlehem

Hebron

Machaerus

Gaza

Masada

Beer-sheba

The Sea of Galilee

Jesus spent much of his ministry – preaching, teaching and healing the sick – in the district of Galilee where most of the people of Palestine lived. The population was particularly large around the Sea of Galilee. Nine or ten towns surrounded the lake at that time, and each had a population of no fewer than 15,000. Today only one remains – Tiberias. The sites of Magdala, Capernaum and Chorazin lie to the north of Tiberias, and those of Bethsaida, Gergesa and Hippos on the eastern side of the lake. But the sites of the other two or three lakeside towns are either uncertain or unknown.

Jesus made Capernaum the headquarters of his Galilean ministry (Matt. 4.12-13). As well as a busy lakeside port, Capernaum was also an important frontier town on the Via Maris, the Roman road from Egypt to Damascus. Peter and Andrew, James and John – the first disciples of Jesus – lived here (Mk. 1.16-20), and so did Matthew, the tax-collector, another disciple (Matt. 9.9).

The Sea of Galilee, which was also called the Lake of Genneseret and the Sea of Tiberias, is only 20 kilometres long and 11 kilometres across at its widest point. But in New Testament times it was famous for its fishing industry. Like some of the disciples, many of the people in the surrounding towns were fishermen. Others worked on the land, especially on the fertile Plain of Gennesaret, which was the market garden of Galilee.

Fishing boat at Tiberias

Church of the Beatitudes overlooking the Sea of Galilee

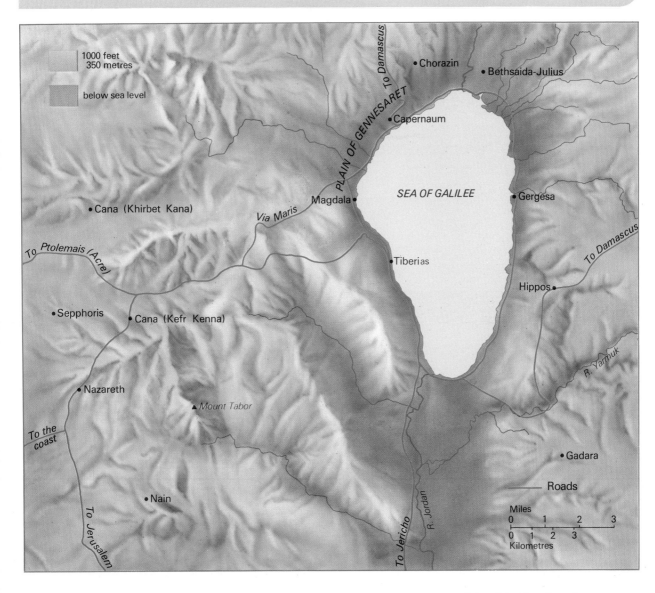

1000 feet
350 metres

below sea level

Chorazin

Bethsaida-Julius

To Damascus

PLAIN OF GENNESARET

Capernaum

Cana (Khirbet Kana)

Magdala

SEA OF GALILEE

Gergesa

Via Maris

To Ptolemais (Acre)

Tiberias

To Damascus

Hippos

Sepphoris

Cana (Kefr Kenna)

R. Yarmuk

Nazareth

▲ Mount Tabor

To the
coast

Gadara

Roads

Nain

Miles
0   1   2   3
0 1   2   3
Kilometres

R. Jordan

To Jericho

To Jerusalem

The synagogue at Capernaum

Mount Tabor — traditional site of the Transfiguration

Jerusalem from the Mount of Olives

At the time of Jesus, Herod the Great had transformed Jerusalem into a splendid city. The plan opposite shows the approximate position of Herod's walls, together with the sites which are known to have existed at that time. The exact course of Herod's northern wall is uncertain. But archaeological evidence indicates that the traditional site of the crucifixion – where the Church of the Holy Sepulchre now stands – lay outside the city walls at the time of Jesus. Today, however, it is situated inside the walls built by the Turks in the 16th century.

Archaeological excavations have also revealed a number of other sites in the city associated with Jesus. Among them is the Antonia Tower, a fortress built by Herod at the north-west corner of the Temple area. This is the traditional site of the Praetorium where Jesus was tried by Pontius Pilate (Jn. 18.28 to 19.16). Excavated remains of the Pool of Bethesda, where Jesus healed a paralysed man (Jn. 5.2. to 9), can also be seen. So, too, can the Pool of Siloam where Jesus healed a blind man (Jn. 9.1-12). This pool was built by Hezekiah when he constructed his famous tunnel through the rock to channel the water from the Gihon Spring into the city (2 Kings 20.20).

Nothing remains of Herod's Temple, which was completely destroyed by Titus in A.D. 70. But the huge Temple area has been preserved, together with sections of its massive retaining walls – including the famous Western, or Wailing, Wall. Since the 7th century, the beautiful Dome of the Rock, a Muslim shrine, has stood on the reputed site of the Temple's altar of burnt-offering.

The Garden of Gethsemane with the Golden Gate behind

The Wailing Wall, the western wall of Herod's Temple

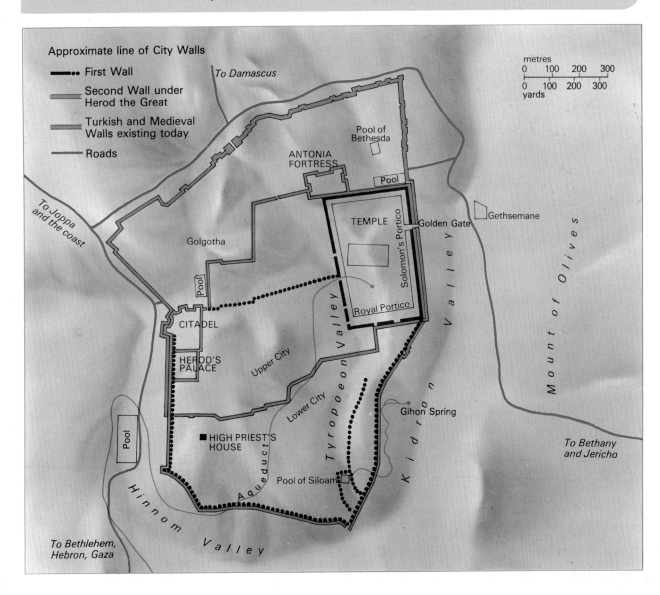

Approximate line of City Walls

- **First Wall**
- Second Wall under Herod the Great
- Turkish and Medieval Walls existing today
- Roads

metres
0   100   200   300
0   100   200   300
yards

To Damascus

Pool of Bethesda

ANTONIA FORTRESS

Pool

To Joppa and the coast

Golgotha

TEMPLE

Solomon's Portico

Golden Gate

Gethsemane

Pool

CITADEL

HEROD'S PALACE

Upper City

Royal Portico

Tyropoeon Valley

Kidron Valley

Mount of Olives

Lower City

Gihon Spring

■ HIGH PRIEST'S HOUSE

Aqueduct

Pool

To Bethany and Jericho

Pool of Siloam

Hinnom Valley

To Bethlehem, Hebron, Gaza

Church of the Holy Sepulchre — site of the crucifixion

The Garden Tomb, Jesus was buried in a similar tomb

Before his Ascension, Jesus told his disciples to remain in Jerusalem until they received the gift of the Holy Spirit. 'You shall receive power when the Holy Spirit has come upon you,' Jesus said, 'and you shall be my witnesses in Jerusalem and in all Judea and Samaria and to the end of the earth' (Acts 1.1-8).

Ten days after the Ascension – on the Jewish Festival of Pentecost – the disciples were filled with the Holy Spirit, as Jesus had promised (Acts 2.1-13). This important event marked the beginning of the Church's life and work, and the disciples immediately began to witness to the resurrection of Jesus in Jerusalem. Like Jesus, they were persecuted by the Jewish religious leaders. But thousands of Jews in Jerusalem were converted to

Philip's Fountain near Hebron

Roman Basilica, Samaria

the Christian faith as a result of their preaching and miracles.

After the martyrdom of Stephen, 'a great persecution arose against the church in Jerusalem' (Acts 8. 1). Apart from the apostles, who at first remained in Jerusalem, the persecuted Christians fled south to Judea, north to Samaria, Phoenicia and Syria, and west to the coastal plain and Cyprus. But wherever they went, the Christians told people about Jesus and made many converts.

Philip, for example, preached in Samaria, baptised an Ethiopian on the road to Gaza, and then preached in the towns of the coastal plain from Azotus to Caesarea (Acts 8.4-40). Later, the apostle Peter also visited the coastal plain, and made converts at Lydda, Joppa and Caesarea (Acts 9.32-43).

When Paul arrived in Damascus after his conversion, he found Christians there (Acts 9.1-9). At Antioch, the capital of Syria, a strong church of Jewish and Gentile converts had also been founded. Antioch soon became a very important Christian centre, and here the disciples were first called Christians (Acts 11.26).

After sending Paul to Tarsus (Acts 9.30), the apostles sent him to Syrian Antioch about A.D. 43 to teach the new converts the Christian faith (Acts 11.19-26). Five years later, about A.D. 47, Paul left Antioch on the first of his three missionary journeys (See pages 50-52). Meanwhile, by A.D. 45, there were Christians in Rome, the capital of the Roman Empire. According to tradition, the apostle Peter first preached the Christian faith in Rome. But the exact date of the Church's foundation here is not known.

Roman harbour at Caesarea

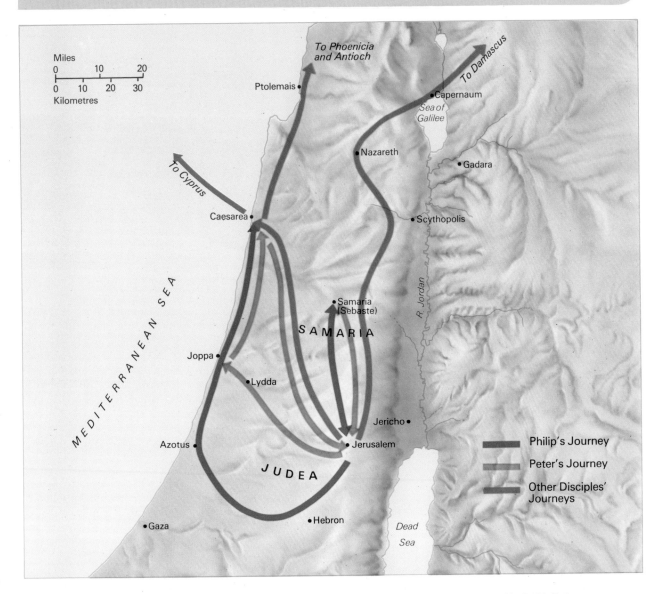

Simon's House, Joppa

St. Peter's Cave Church at Antakya (Antioch), Turkey

Paul set out on his first missionary journey in the spring of A.D. 47, accompanied by Barnabas and John Mark (Acts 13 and 14). From Antioch in Syria they went to Seleucia, and sailed to Salamis in Cyprus. They crossed the island to Paphos where the Roman proconsul, Sergius Paulus, was converted. From Paphos the party sailed to Attalia (Antalya) in Asia Minor, and went on to Perga in Pamphylia. Here, perhaps because he was homesick, John Mark suddenly returned home to Jerusalem. But Paul and Barnabas continued their journey

Perga gate at Antalya (Attalia), Turkey

Roman Gymnasium at Salamis, Cyprus

inland to Antioch of Pisidia, Iconium (Konya), Lystra and Derbe. Then they retraced their steps to Attalia. From here they sailed back to Seleucia, and returned to Antioch in the summer of A.D. 49. In spite of much opposition to their preaching, Paul and Barnabas succeeded in making many converts, and Paul's Letter to the Galatians was probably written to the churches they founded in south Galatia.

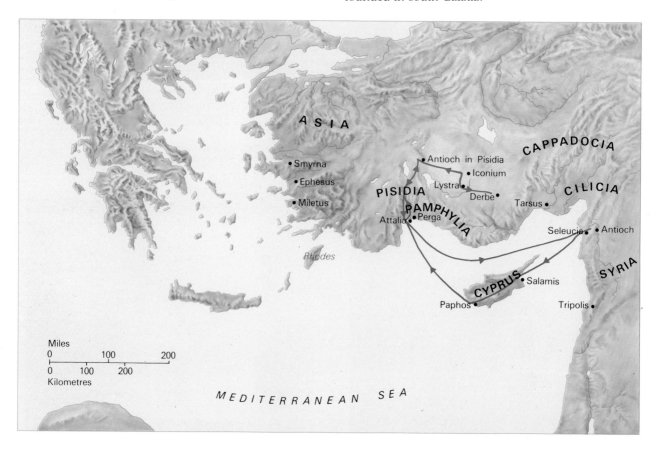

Paul left Antioch in Syria on his second missionary journey in the spring of A.D. 50, accompanied by Silas (Acts 15.36 to 18.22). From Antioch they travelled through Syria and Cilicia, and then visited the churches in south Galatia founded on Paul's first journey. At Lystra they were joined by Timothy, a recent young convert.

In Galatia, Paul changed his proposed itinerary. Instead of preaching in Asia and Bithynia, the party

The Parthenon in Athens, Greece

Main street of Roman Philippi, Greece

travelled through Mysia to Troas where Luke, the author of Acts, joined them. From Troas they sailed to Neapolis (Kavalla) in Macedonia, and founded the first churches in Europe – at Philippi, Thessalonica and Beroea. Jewish opposition forced Paul to leave Beroea, and he went on to Athens and then to Corinth. After spending eighteen months in Corinth, Paul returned to Antioch in the summer of A.D. 53.

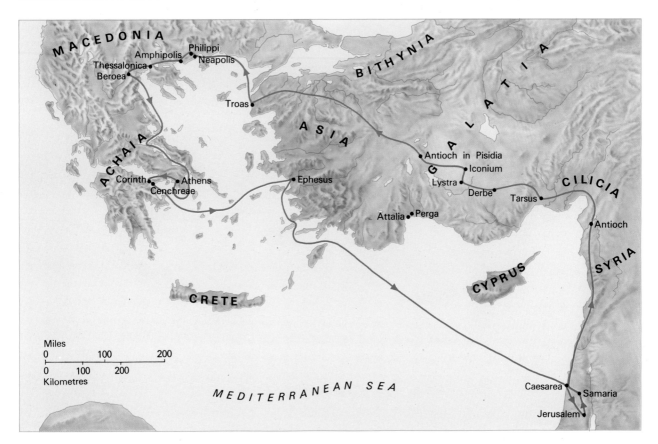

Paul left Antioch on his last and longest missionary journey in the summer of A.D. 53 (Acts 18.23 to 21.16). This time Paul travelled by himself and, after visiting the churches in south Galatia, he went to Ephesus where he stayed for over two years. During this time churches were founded not only in Ephesus, but also in other parts of Asia. When a riot brought Paul's work at Ephesus to an end, he went to Macedonia and Achaia (Greece).

Remains of Roman baths at Troas, Turkey

The theatre of Ephesus, Turkey

Paul was planning to sail from Greece to Syria when he heard of a Jewish plot to kill him. So he returned to Macedonia, and sailed from Neapolis. At Troas Paul was joined by delegates from various churches, who accompanied him to Jerusalem with a collection for the poor Christians. They arrived in the summer of AD. 57 and, as Paul expected, Jewish hostility soon led to his arrest and imprisonment.

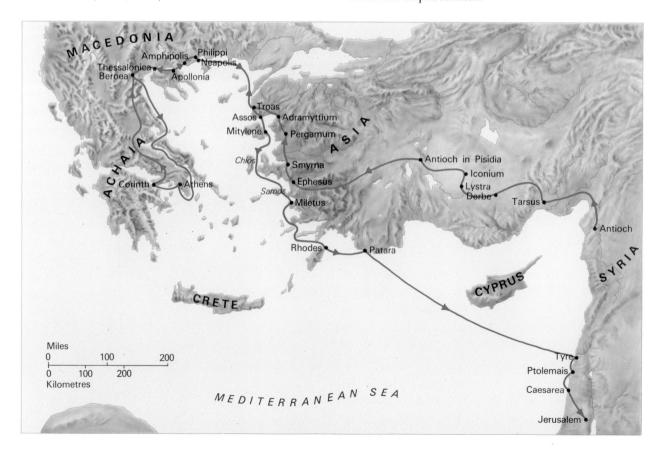

The Romans arrested Paul during a Jewish riot in Jerusalem, and sent him to Caesarea where he was imprisoned for two years – from A.D. 57-59 (Acts 21.27 to 26.32). When Paul appealed to be tried by the emperor, he was sent to Rome under escort by sea (Acts 27 to 28.16). He sailed from Caesarea, in August A.D. 59, to Myra in Lycia where he changed to a ship bound for Italy. But south of Crete a violent storm arose which wrecked the ship – without loss of life – on the island of Malta.

Pyramid of Cestius in Rome, Italy

Statue of St. Paul, Malta

After spending three months in Malta, Paul continued his journey under escort by sea to Puteoli (Pozzuoli) in Italy. Then he travelled overland to Rome where he arrived in February A.D. 60. Paul remained a prisoner in Rome for two years. Then, according to tradition, he was released and made further journeys before his final arrest and execution in Rome about A.D. 67.

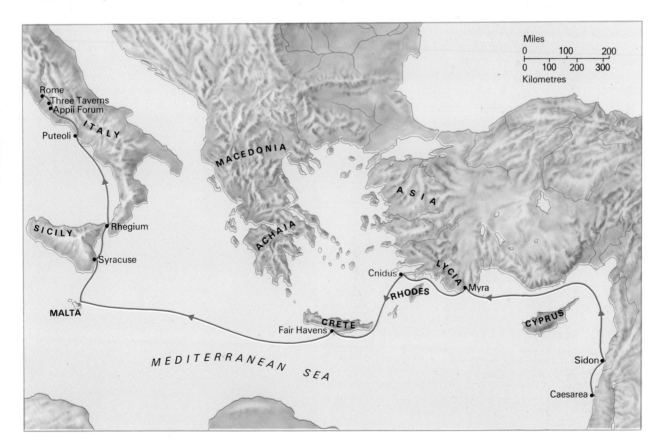

St. John's Basilica at Ephesus, Turkey

Roman aqueduct at Smyrna (Izmir), Turkey

The spread of the Church to Asia Minor was mainly, but not entirely, due to the work of St. Paul. He certainly founded churches in south Galatia – at Antioch in Pisidia, Iconium, Lystra and Derbe – and probably in Pamphylia as well, for example, at Perga (Acts 14.25). Paul was also the first to establish the Church in the Roman Province of Asia. But he was helped by Barnabas, Silas and Timothy, who travelled with him in Asia Minor, and also by other Christian workers. Among those who helped him at Ephesus were Priscilla and Aquila (Acts 18.18), Gaius and Aristarchus (Acts 19.29), and Tychicus and Trophimus (Acts 29.4).

From Ephesus, Paul also sent out workers to other cities in the Province of Asia where churches were established, for example, at Colossae, Hierapolis and Laodicea (Col. 4.7-17). We know, too, that there were Christians at Troas and Miletus, and probably at Assos as well (Acts 20.5-17). From St. John's Letters to the Seven Churches of Asia in the Book of Revelation (Rev. 2 and 3) we learn that, towards the end of the 1st century A.D., there were well-established churches at Smyrna, Pergamum, Thyatira, Sardis and Philadelphia, as well as at Ephesus and Laodicea.

But other missionaries – apart from Paul and his helpers – were also founding churches in Asia Minor during the 1st century A.D. – in areas which Paul did not visit. For the First Letter of Peter is addressed to Christians in Pontus, Cappadocia and Bithynia, as well as Galatia and Asia (1 Peter 1.1). By the end of the 1st century A.D., therefore, the Church had spread through most of Asia Minor, which later became an important area of Christianity in the east.

Temple of Trajan in Pergamum, Turkey

Remains of early Christian Basilica in Thyatira, Turkey

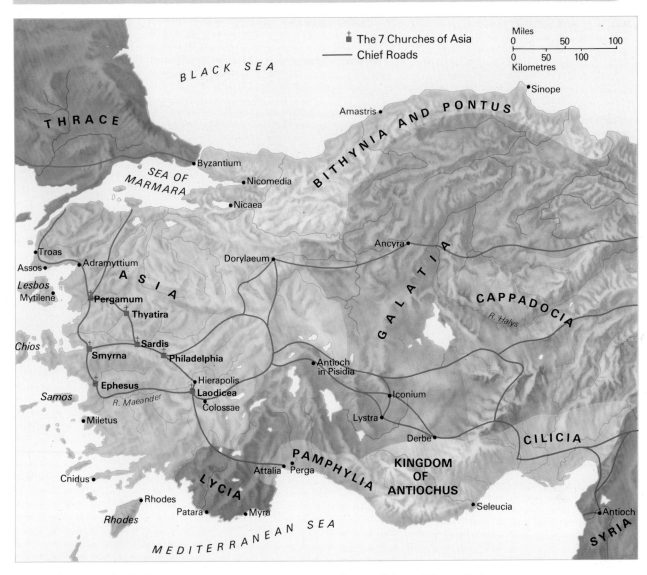

BLACK SEA

THRACE

BITHYNIA AND PONTUS

· Sinope

Amastris ·

· Byzantium

SEA OF MARMARA

· Nicomedia

· Nicaea

Ancyra ·

GALATIA

Dorylaeum ·

CAPPADOCIA

R. Halys

· Troas

Assos ·

· Adramyttium

Lesbos

Mytilene ·

A S I A

Pergamum

Thyatira

Chios

Sardis

Smyrna

Philadelphia

Ephesus

Hierapolis

Laodicea

Colossae

Samos

R. Maeander

· Antioch in Pisidia

· Iconium

Lystra ·

· Miletus

Derbe ·

CILICIA

KINGDOM OF ANTIOCHUS

PAMPHYLIA

Cnidus ·

LYCIA

Attalia · Perga

Rhodes ·

· Rhodes

Patara ·

· Myra

· Seleucia

· Antioch

SYRIA

MEDITERRANEAN SEA

Legend:
- The 7 Churches of Asia
- Chief Roads

Miles
0   50   100
0   50   100
Kilometres

Temple of Artemis in Sardis, Turkey

Statue of Diana at Ephesus, Turkey

Time chart for the New Testament Period

B.C.	PALESTINE	NEW TESTAMENT EVENTS	THE ROMAN EMPIRE
6		Birth of Jesus	
4	Death of Herod the Great. His kingdom divided between his sons. Archelaus ethnarch of Judea; Antipas tetrarch of Galilee and Perea; Philip tetrarch of Iturea and Trachonitis.		
A.D.			
6	Deposition of Archelaus and appointment of Roman Procurator.		
14			Death of Augustus and accession of Tiberius.
26	Pontius Pilate appointed.	Beginning of Jesus's ministry.	
29–30		Crucifixion, Resurrection, and Ascension of Jesus. Pentecost: the Church begins.	
32–33		Martyrdom of Stephen and conversion of St. Paul.	
34	Death of Herod Philip		
35		Paul's first visit to Jerusalem.	
36	Removal of Pontius Pilate.		
37			Caligula
			Claudius
41	Herod Agrippa I King of Judea.		
43		Paul in Antioch. James the Apostle martyred.	
44	Death of Herod Agrippa.		
45–46		Paul's second visit to Jerusalem.	
47–49		First missionary journey.	
49		Third visit to Jerusalem for Council.	
50–53		Second missionary journey.	
50	Herod Agrippa II.		
52	Felix appointed Procurator of Judea.		
53		Paul's fourth visit to Jerusalem.	
53–57		Third missionary journey.	
54			Nero
57		Fifth visit to Jerusalem.	
57–59		Paul's imprisonment in Caesarea.	
59	Festus appointed Procurator.	Paul appeals to Caesar. Voyage to Rome.	
60–62		Paul's imprisonment in Rome.	
61		Death of James, the Lord's brother in Jerusalem.	
64	Florus the Procurator.		Great fire in Rome; persecution of Christians.
66	First Jewish Revolt.		
67		St. Peter's and St. Paul's martyrdom	
68			Death of Nero
70	Jerusalem destroyed by Titus		
81–96		Persecution of Christians.	Domitian
98			Trajan
100		Death of St. John the Apostle.	
117			Hadrian
132	Second Jewish Revolt.		
135	Jerusalem rebuilt by Hadrian and renamed Aelia Capitolina.		
138			Death of Hadrian.

(Dates are approximate)

Remains of the city wall of Philadelphia, Turkey

Aqueduct pipes in Laodicea, Turkey

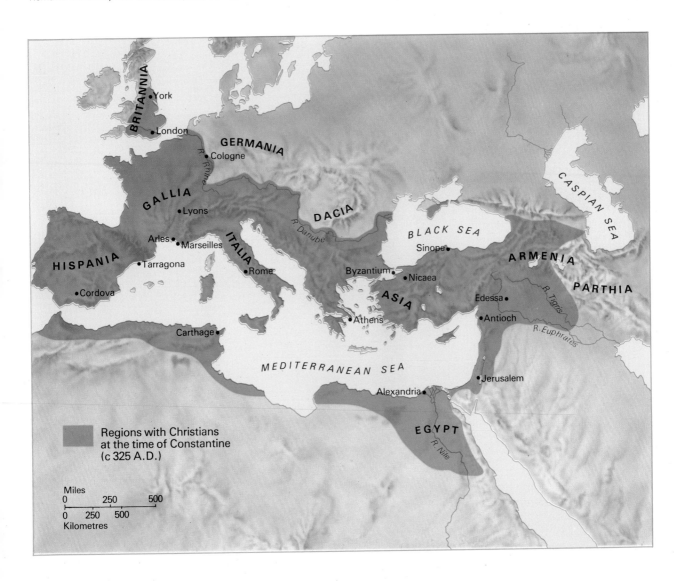

BRITANNIA
York
London
GERMANIA
Cologne
R. Rhine
GALLIA
Lyons
Arles
Marseilles
ITALIA
HISPANIA
Tarragona
Rome
Cordova
Carthage
DACIA
R. Danube
BLACK SEA
Sinope
Byzantium
Nicaea
ASIA
Athens
CASPIAN SEA
ARMENIA
PARTHIA
Edessa
R. Tigris
Antioch
R. Euphrates
MEDITERRANEAN SEA
Jerusalem
Alexandria
R. Nile
EGYPT

Regions with Christians
at the time of Constantine
(c 325 A.D.)

Miles
0   250   500
0   250   500
Kilometres

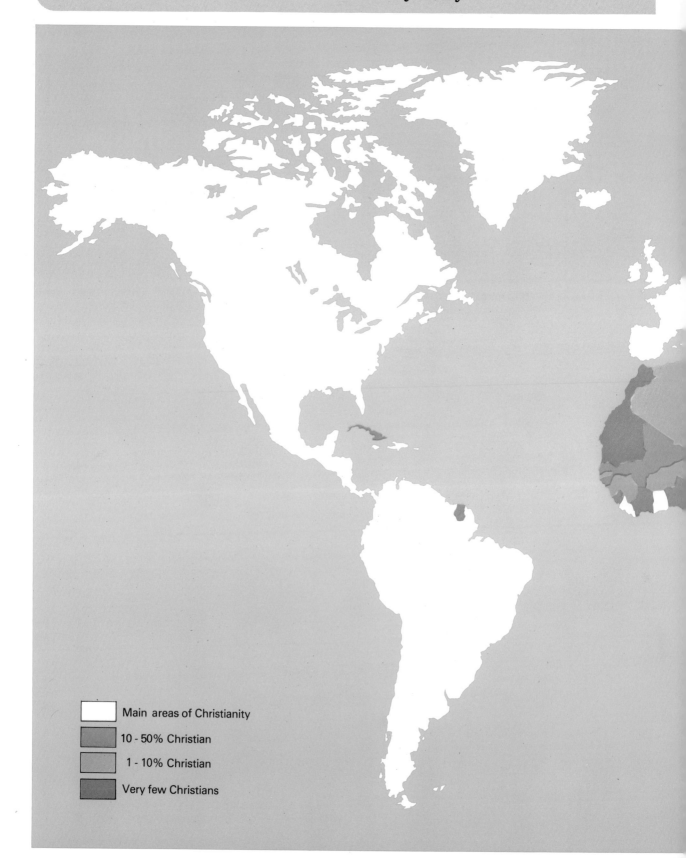

Main areas of Christianity

10 - 50% Christian

1 - 10% Christian

Very few Christians

The maps on pages 62-63 and 64 show only the most important archaeological sites in Bible lands. For since the 19th century numerous Biblical and other ancient sites have been excavated, and new sites are continually being discovered and excavated.

In 1964, for example, Italian archaeologists, who had been making a survey in north Syria, decided to excavate a huge mound known as Tell Mardikh, 56 kilometres south of Aleppo. Nothing was known about the site. But four years later – in 1968 – an inscribed statue was unearthed which identified the site as Ebla. Little was known about this obscure ancient city. But in 1975 the archaeologists made a sensational discovery. In a room near the entrance to a royal palace, which had been destroyed by fire c. 2250 B.C., they found more than 15,000 clay tablets covered with cuneiform writing.

Excavations in progress near the Temple area, Jerusalem

Jericho — defence tower dating from Neolithic times

been founded much later. So, too, are names known to us from Genesis such as Abraham, Ishmael and Esau. This has caused the biggest surprise amongst Biblical scholars because the tablets were written four or five hundred years before the proposed dates of the Patriarchs. The excavations at Ebla, therefore, will not only open up a new chapter in the history of the Middle East, but also have a profound effect on Biblical scholarship.

Ebla is but one example of the numerous archaeological sites which are adding to knowledge of the Bible and its historical background. Another is Ugarit (Ras-Shamra), an impressive site on the Mediterranean coast in north Syria, where excavations have been carried out for the past forty years. Among the many important

Excavations south-west of the Temple wall, Jerusalem

They were the official state records of the Kingdom of Ebla between c. 2400 B.C. and 2250 B.C.

Most of the tablets record details of Ebla's administration, commerce and foreign relationships. They reveal that, during the third millenium B.C., Ebla was the capital of a Middle Eastern empire and civilisation which was previously unknown. Among the other tablets are thirty-two bilingual dictionaries in Sumerian and Eblaite, a previously unknown west Semitic language. But most intriguing of all are the similarities between some of the tablets and parts of the Old Testament written more than a millenium later.

There are stories of the Creation and Flood, for example, similar to those in the book of Genesis. Also mentioned are names of cities in Palestine – such as Hazor, Megiddo and Jerusalem – which were thought to have

Excavations at Ur which show evidence of the Flood

Staircase to the Temple of Augustus, Samaria

discoveries made here were thousands of clay tablets from the libraries of two Canaanite temples dating from the 15th-14th centuries B.C. They were written in a previously unknown alphabetic script of thirty cuneiform signs, known as Ugaritic, which played an important part in the later development of writing. Some of the texts record stories about the Canaanite gods and goddesses such as El, Baal and Asherah. They have provided important new knowledge about the Canaanite religion, which had such a great influence on the Israelites. The high standard of Canaanite civilisation and culture also had a great influence on the Israelites as the excavations of Canaanite cities in Palestine have revealed, for example, at Gezer, Megiddo and Hazor.

Among the most important excavations in Palestine in recent times are those at Qumran where the first Dead Sea Scrolls were found in 1947. Others include the late Dame Kathleen Kenyon's excavations at Jericho in the 1950s and Jerusalem in the 1960s, which have completely altered our knowledge of the history and development of these sites. For example, she discovered that Jericho was occupied as early as c. 9000 B.C., and that the Jebusite city of Jerusalem – captured by David c. 1000 B.C. – was situated on the steep eastern slopes of Mount Ophel.

Qumran Cave 4 where the first Dead Sea Scrolls were found.

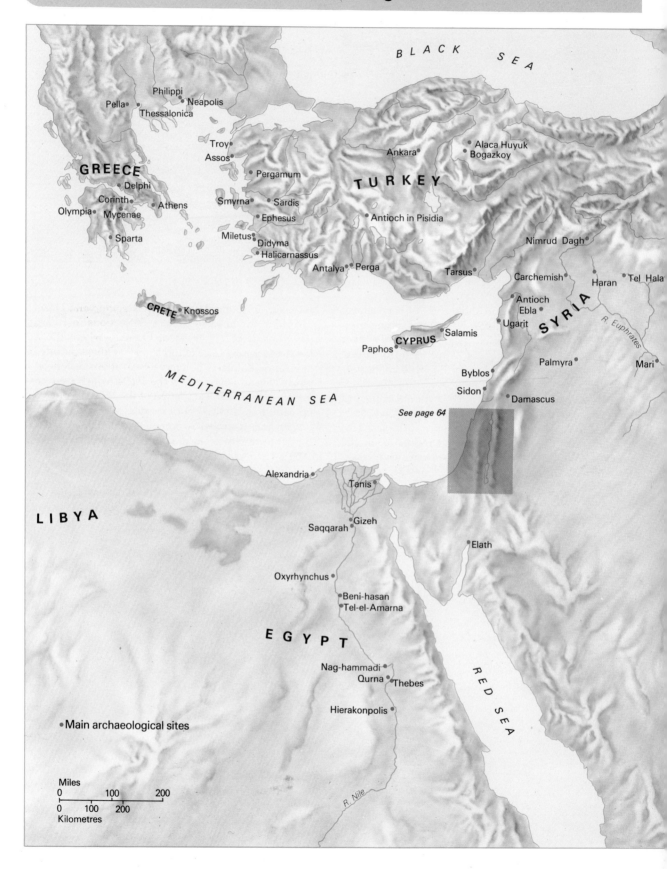

BLACK SEA

GREECE

Pella
Philippi
Neapolis
Thessalonica
Troy
Assos
Delphi
Corinth
Athens
Olympia
Mycenae
Sparta
Pergamum
Smyrna
Sardis
Ephesus
Miletus
Didyma
Halicarnassus
Antalya
Perga

TURKEY

Ankara
Alaca Huyuk
Bogazkoy
Antioch in Pisidia
Nimrud Dagh
Carchemish
Haran
Tel Hala
Tarsus
Antioch
Ebla
Ugarit

SYRIA

R. Euphrates

Palmyra
Mari

CRETE Knossos

CYPRUS
Paphos
Salamis

Byblos
Sidon
Damascus

MEDITERRANEAN SEA

See page 64

Alexandria
Tanis

LIBYA

Saqqarah
Gizeh

Elath

Oxyrhynchus

Beni-hasan
Tel-el-Amarna

EGYPT

Nag-hammadi
Qurna
Thebes

Hierakonpolis

RED SEA

•Main archaeological sites

Miles
0   100   200
0   100   200
Kilometres

R. Nile

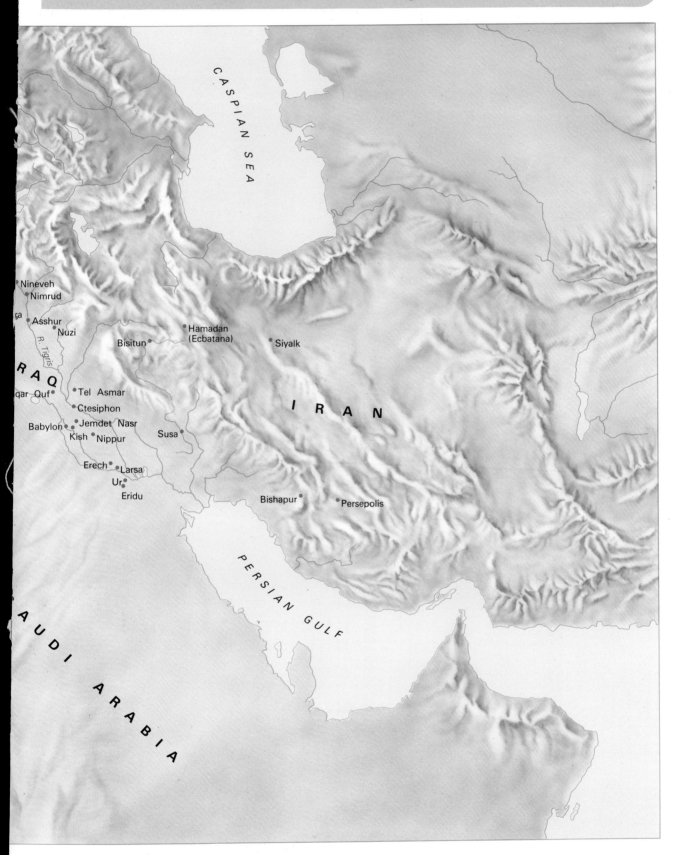

CASPIAN SEA

Nineveh
Nimrud
Asshur
Nuzi
Hamadan
(Ecbatana)
Bisitun
Siyalk

R. Tigris

I R A N

R A Q

qar Quf
Tel Asmar
Ctesiphon
Jemdet Nasr
Babylon
Kish
Nippur
Susa
Erech
Larsa
Ur
Eridu

Bishapur
Persepolis

AUDI ARABIA

PERSIAN GULF

Palestine: Archaeological Sites

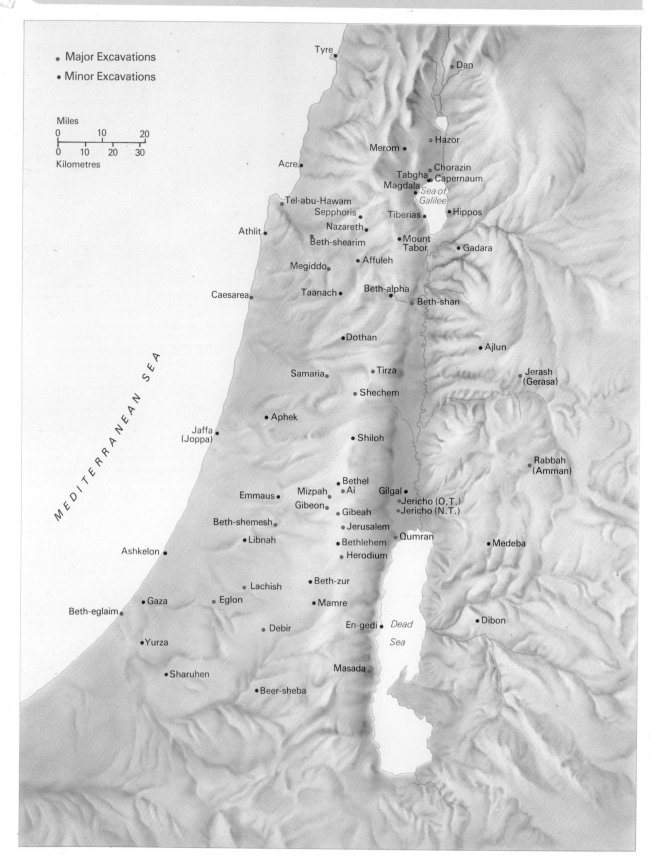

- Major Excavations
- Minor Excavations

Miles
0   10   20
0 10 20 30
Kilometres

Tyre

Dan

Hazor

Merom

Acre

Chorazin
Tabgha Capernaum
Magdala
Sea of
Galilee

Tel-abu-Hawam
Sepphoris
Tiberias
Hippos

Athlit
Nazareth
Beth-shearim
Mount
Tabor
Gadara

Megiddo
Affuleh

Caesarea
Taanach
Beth-alpha
Beth-shan

Dothan

Ajlun

Samaria
Tirza

Shechem

Jerash
(Gerasa)

Aphek

Jaffa
(Joppa)
Shiloh

MEDITERRANEAN SEA

Rabbah
(Amman)

Bethel
Emmaus
Mizpah
Ai
Gilgal
Gibeon
Jericho (O.T.)
Jericho (N.T.)
Gibeah
Beth-shemesh
Jerusalem
Libnah
Bethlehem
Qumran
Ashkelon
Herodium
Medeba

Beth-zur
Lachish
Gaza
Eglon
Mamre
Beth-eglaim
En-gedi
Dead
Sea
Dibon
Debir
Yurza

Masada
Sharuhen

Beer-sheba

Printed in Hong Kong by Wing King Tong Co Ltd